REFLECTIONS ON LIFE IN
THE EXIT LANE

HOWARD M. STIEN

HM Stien

A BOOK OF DAYS. A CELEBRATION OF YEARS.

Seventy years is the span of life,

eighty if our strength holds ... we spend our years

as a tale being told under the watchful eye of God ...

the hurrying years pass quickly and are forgotten.

PSALM 90

Surely a bit of remembering won't hurt.

© 2008 Howard M Stien
Second printing
ISBN: 0-9707334-2-9

All Rights Reserved. No part of this publication may be reproduced, stored in a retrieval system, or transmitted in any form or by any means, electronic, mechanical, photocopying, recording, or otherwise without the express written permission of the copyright owner, except for purposes of critical review.

For information, contact the author at HMStien.com
or 509 466-5449

Also by Howard Stien:
STUMP HOUSE STORIES
THE IMPROBABLE PROFESSOR

Published by Stump House Books
Spokane, WA 99218, USA
509 466-5449

Cover photo - © Jeremy Edwards: istockphoto.com
Book design - Kindred Creative Services - 509 466-2208

Printed in the USA

To Pat

Come live with me and be my love

And find some new pleasure prove

Of golden sand and crystal brooks

With silken lines and silver hooks.

- JOHN DONNE

Contents

PROLOGUE 1

APRIL 3

MAY 37

JUNE 75

JULY 107

AUGUST 139

SEPTEMBER 171

OCTOBER 211

NOVEMBER 247

DECEMBER 285

JANUARY 319

FEBRUARY 353

MARCH 397

APRIL AGAIN 433

INDEX 445

Prologue

The Old Testament poet enjoins us to number our days. There is something bittersweet about this bit of psaltery. We are reminded that *We spend our years as a tale being told under the watchful eye of God*. We are further reminded when the end to all this counting might be approaching. *Seventy years is the span of life, eighty if our strength holds—the hurrying years pass quickly and are forgotten*, the Psalmist writes. (I don't like this being forgotten bit.)

The Psalmist also writes, *Teach us to count our days so that we may apply our hearts unto wisdom*. Or in contemporary words, *Teach us to order our days that we may enter the gate of wisdom*. (I like this part.) The confluence of age and wisdom is a persistent theme in the literature of all ages. It could still happen.

To count our days seems to be instinctive. We humans tend to do that even in oblivion to the biblical injunction. Some may celebrate birthdays without recognizing that life is a gift and the passing years are an extension of that gift. It's when we acknowledge that life is a gift from God we begin to understand the point of all this palaver about counting. I assume it means not only are we to count our days but we are to pay some attention to whether the passing years count or have counted for anything.

Although the ancient poet doesn't indicate when one should begin to count one's days, the context of his words implies that to do so is good, especially for octogenarian souls. Having by virtue of strength or good fortune reached the lofty levels of which he speaks, I have resolved to number (count) each of the remaining days of my sojourn with an inscription. To what end this daily baring my soul or scouring my mind, I am uncertain. If perchance some wisdom emerges in these days, I would be pleased and intend to watch for it closely.

This endeavor, however, should in no way infer that the prior 29,120 unnoted days of my earthly sojourn were devoid of significance, joy, or consequence. Those were the good old days—recounted or uncounted days perhaps—through which flowed all the accumulated stuff of life.

As the days accumulate, the ratio of past to future shifts disproportionately to the past, and recounting days may indeed take preeminence in my daily musing about existence.

Therefore, on this final day of the final year of the eighth decade of this journey, pondering the future in the context of a memorable past, I begin my quest for wisdom. Should some wisdom emerge in these days yet to be counted, all will be well with my soul.

HMS

April

APRIL 11

In the beginning

On this day in April, eighty years ago, I was born. Nothing really unusual about neither the date nor the occasion, perhaps. Worldwide, I suppose, a number of children were born that April day, but in a very personal way the day was special. Of course, without the unique events that presented the world to me there would be no days for me to number. But the day was for my parents extraordinary. My arrival was not unanticipated but that of my twin was totally unexpected. (It was 1926.) It could be said that he was the anticipated one and I was unexpected, but the records show that I was the first to arrive.

Our being twins lent a special dimension to our birthday celebrations. It was on those occasions that the individuality of our lives momentarily became less significant. Our lives always came together on this calendar day. It was then that our stories became one again.

We counted years together—in the Psalmist's notation, threescore and two. Those were good years (good in all the best meanings of the word). Since then a sadness lingers near the surface on this day in April, as I give thanks for the bonus years I have been granted but mourn his absence in them. I wonder if I accepted all that was offered to me from the gift of his presence. I miss the guy.

I count the days alone.

APRIL 12

Pinch Day Poets

Traditions are, I suppose, as varied as the families who sustain them. In our family today is Pinch Day, a personal and uncommon custom. I can't remember when I first learned of or experienced the dubious pleasure of this affectionate pinch. Nor can I remember when anyone in our family was not greeted on the day after one's birthday with the words "Happy Pinch Day" and the well-intended but questionable gesture of affection. The origin of this practice is unclear but I am certain that our parents, who I assume learned it from theirs, introduced the custom to us. Our children, although less faithful in observing the practice, adopted it from us.

Pinch Days, as a rule, are less memorable than birthdays. I have no clear recollection of my 18th birthday, but my memories of Pinch Day that year are indelible. My parents accompanied me to the local railroad station to meet the 4:30 AM mail train. The world was at war and I, just turned 18, was on my way to report for duty. Frivolity was not in the air. The day was devoid of celebratory pinches. There were only prolonged hugs of affection and concern from my usually stoic Scandinavian parents. It affirmed my suspicions that they did indeed love me.

That was then. Today was not about pinches, although the custom was duly noted by Pat. It was about poets. Pat and I went to our local independent bookstore to listen to poets read their favorite lines. There were two of them. One was a dear

7

friend, serious and devoted to the study of the inner life. She was attuned to the turmoil in lives of hurting but rejoicing people. The other was a big fellow, jovial, and larger than I thought a poet needed to be. He looked out at the sky, the mountains, the trees, the river, and the lake—somewhat detached I thought.

The contrast pinched a bit.

APRIL 13

Hey, Smokey

"You smell like smoke," Pat said to me today when I returned from my yearly trek to the ranch to assist with the cattle branding operation. She was right. The eye-searing, acrid smoke from hair scorched by red-hot irons clings to one's clothes with tenacity unmatched by smoke from any source — perhaps an unwelcome reminder of the pitiless practice of burning one's mark onto the hide of innocent critters.

My annual excursion to participate in this ritual began thirty-five years ago when I was recruited to assist a young rancher, who had inherited the responsibility of the entire ranch by the untimely death of his father. Although I was accustomed to working with cattle—my father was a dairy farmer when I was a youth—I was only vaguely familiar with a beef cattle operation of this scale.

My first assignment was wrestling unwilling calves into the restraining device where experienced guys proceeded with emasculation, dehorning, branding, tagging and inoculation, none of which are gentle procedures but at which in subsequent years I had my turn. My initiation in the chutes was physically demanding and exceedingly untidy. My promotion toward the head of the critters proceeded on schedule and now (with deference to age, of course) I have advanced to the head of the sequence of tasks as well as to the head of the animal. I have but one advancement yet to master—that of headcounter. Ranchers don't count animals. They just count heads. Next year I will record the number and gender of the critters as they exit the chute. Working up front is less exciting, but it is also much less untidy.

What began as actual help has evolved into tradition. My friends would have me believe my presence is vital, but in reality my contribution to this annual caper these days tends more towards the symbolic.

Life is like that!

APRIL 14

Actuarial Reality

My reading of the New Testament indicates that the Israelites of the time had few good things to say about tax collectors. It's the time of year when the still-hated tax collector looms large at our door. It has been said that the two things from which one never escapes are death and taxes. They continue concomitantly until we stand before the Great Accountant in the Sky.

Our tax accountant (a likeable young man, by the way) stopped by this evening for some additional numbers to complete our annual admissions to the IRS. He has the doubly dubious duty of minimizing our obligation as well as keeping us honest. A few years ago in a conversation with him about the former, he wondered whether we might withdraw all of our tax-sheltered funds, pay the taxes, reinvest the remainder and recover the cost of the tax. But reconsidering he said, "Actually, actuarial reality precludes that. You only have thirteen years left." In other words, we were already too old.

The idea of actuarial reality has become a handy response to solicitors who would sell us long-term investments. A telemarketer called last evening offering us a three-year extension to our Time Magazine subscription for one-third of the regular price. An attractive offer, I submit, for 20-year-olds. "Not a good idea given our actuarial reality," I told him. Perplexed, he asked what I meant. "At our age we begin to question the purchase of a new pair of shoes," I replied. "Oh!" he responded, as the lights went on.

I like the irony of "already too old" being a useful dodge.

APRIL 15

Near Elderly

One year ago this day Pat and I were coasting along, blissfully I suppose, taking for granted the reasonably good health that has been ours. So much so that our references to our demographic niche avoids all mention of old, aged, and elderly.

When pushed toward reality we would admit to *near elderly*. What engenders my reluctance to identify with folks our age (Pat's also, but she doesn't fret about it as much as I) is the predilection of that group to make aches, pains, pills, surgeries, and diminishing capacities major topics of conversation. The common casual question, "How are you?" seems to demand a detailed answer.

We, like many of the near elderly, had been cruising in the slow lane giving little conscious thought to the imminent exit lane when we were suddenly reminded that our exemptions from mortality were temporary. In the emergency room that evening Pat's doctor said, "Except for a few fortunate circumstances, we would not be having this conversation."

Today we are back on the road ever more grateful for the favor to keep counting our days.

APRIL 16

Stumped

Throughout the years I built several play stations for our children and grandchildren, often with the suspicion that my fantasy with these creations exceeded that of the kids. The latest and the most creative of these constructions in my assessment was The Stump House. Initially envisioned as a tree house, we built it on a large, five-foot-high Ponderosa stump. It was popular with our grandchildren, great grandchildren, our neighbor's grandchildren and numerous other visiting kids. We actually published a collection of children's stories set in the tree house built on a stump.

The life expectancy of a stump was not a concern when we built the house. "A stump is a tree with its head cut off" is a quote from the book that suggests the stump was already dead when we built the house. Nevertheless. attacked by insects and fungus the stump eventually failed and the playhouse now lists precariously unsafe for child play.

What to do about that emerges as the decision of the day. Dismantle the structure and with it the legend? Settle it on the ground and lessen its novelty? Cut down a tree to make a stump? Create a manmade stump? I have been trying to envision a manmade stump.

Only God can make a tree, the poet declares. Does it follow then that only God can make a stump?

I am going to quit for the day and think about it.

APRIL 17

Obviosities

Ordinarily notions like *Life is a gift given to us incrementally* don't occupy a lot of mental space. Such truisms are usually dismissed as obviosities (my word for things that are obvious). But some of these banalities merit closer scrutiny.

What if the converse were true? *As sure as night follows day* is a well-worn expression denoting high probability. But I think it's true only for folks born during the day. I was born during nighttime and had survived several hours of darkness before I encountered daylight. More true for me would be: *As sure as day follows night.* I don't wish for those first significant hours to be discounted before the counting began. I wonder if folks who have difficulty remembering whether they are coming or going may be confused about when it all began. How many times have you been told *You can't have this without that* when it may be more true that *You can't have that without this?* One can't have days without nights anymore than one can have nights without days.

But back to the notion that life is incremental. Whether those increments are days or nights was left uncertain by the Psalmist in his encouragement to number our days. In reality, sleeping and waking, as we experience both, do indeed leave the impression that starting and stopping is the way life is lived. Or is it stopping and starting? The ancient poet's reference to days notwithstanding, life seems to me to be seamless.

Is that not obvious?

APRIL 18

Paralogue (a parenthesis)

While contemplating my intention to honor the Psalmist's prompting by writing a daily blurb, it occurred to me that the days to be counted are the days yet to come. The days gone by have, in a sense, already been counted. I am counting on the hope that the poet will not be offended if I recount some of the more memorable days among those already counted.

In a life span of fourscore years each calendar day will have occurred eighty times, which affords one eighty opportunities to make any particular day in the annual cycle count for something. Some days acquire a significance that eclipses all subsequent appearances of that date.

It is entirely possible that on some, if not most of the 365 days in all of their annual manifestations, nothing of consequence happened except that one received another increment in the gift of life, a day to be cherished for that reason alone. The Psalmist (probably while counting his days) wrote, *This is the day that the Lord has made. Rejoice and be glad in it.* That is true of all one's days and may indeed be what the writer had in mind when he wrote, *Count your days.* At the risk of adding to the intent of Holy Script, I will add the words "all of them" and be reminded that there are days in everyone's repertoire that merit recounting.

Surely, a bit of recounting can't hurt.

APRIL 19

Musical Potpourri

My preference in music tends toward country western tunes. It was a natural predilection for the farm boy that I was. My appreciation for classical music, however, has been learned if not earned. It has been nurtured by a long, continuing exposure to symphonic concerts motivated largely by Pat's wish that I acquire some measure of culture. I have my favorite composers—Mozart and Gershwin—and some recognizable tunes. There are a small number of classical pieces that break into song on occasion. I like those the best.

After a day marked mostly by routine, Pat and I attended a musical event, which was delightfully different from the usual. It happened in an elegant ballroom in our city's recently restored, 1890 historic hotel.

Rich folks sat at tables on the main floor and sipped wine and munched hors d'oeuvres. The rest of us were seated along the balcony rail affording us an unobstructed view of the musicians and unique opportunity to look down on wealthier patrons.

The program was a potpourri of music performed by small ensembles. A quintet of brass players performed a number of typically noisy brass pieces by Handel and others. I rather enjoyed the brevity of their program. I suppose it is redundant to say two bassoonists played a bassoon duet, but that is just what they did. I think I now know why a lot of bassoon duets have not been written. >>>

After an overlong intermission the standard string quartet took the stage and played what I, in my musical naïveté, would call a standard string quartet program. I divided my time between listening to the music and watching the artists. I envy Pat's ability to do both at the same time.

We closed the evening with some non-musical palaver over beer and nachos at our favorite post-concert hangout and arrived at home in time for the news.

Overall, I think the evening inched my musical acculturation up a degree or two.

APRIL 20

Easter

In my repertoire of memories, few days—other than the day I met Pat—take up more space than Easter. In our large but close-knit family Easter was always a momentous time in our annual cycle of special days. It signified new life, both literally and spiritually. The latter because, after weeks of snowbound restricted travel in mid-continent winter, our family would again take up our practice of Sunday worship at the neighborhood Lutheran church. I was steeped in the beliefs, biblical traditions, and Lutheran rituals of Easter from early Sunday school through confirmation, where I learned the answers to questions I had not yet asked, the significance of which occurred to me later.

There were contemporary cultural traditions—Easter bunny and colored eggs from our own hens, Easter dinner featuring ham from our own pigs (poor critters) and Easter finery depicted in the popular song, *Put on your Easter bonnet with all the frills upon it and join the Easter parade*. We didn't have a parade. That was city stuff and we were farm folk. But it was a time of hope dampened only on occasion by a late winter snowstorm. I remember it snowed on Pat's Easter bonnet our first Easter together.

I carried the influence of this tradition with me when I moved around the country and abroad with fellow soldiers during our war. (Every generation has had its war.) I was in Italy when Easter came around in 1945. It was an exceptionally beautiful spring day and we, our bomber crew and a couple dozen other crews, were sent to drop bombs in Yugoslavia. The skies were cloudless. The scene below was dotted with picturesque mountain villages and our bombs fell on a bridge across a river flowing peacefully near one of them. Our mission was uneventful. There was no enemy resistance. I pondered the strategic value of the bridge.

When we returned to base and were, as was the practice, debriefed and awarded a shot of bourbon allegedly to quiet us down, I wondered whether anyone other than I realized it was Easter Sunday. I inquired and learned that there was to be a religious service at a nondescript building on base. The service was quite perfunctory and as nondescript as the building. No mention of Easter or of God, as I recall.

Bewildered, I wandered back to my tent disquieted, not so much about the service as the thought that our bombs may have fallen on Easter worshippers in the village near the bridge.

APRIL 21

Dismissed

"I understand that you are going home today," the nurse said when she entered my hospital room at 5:30 AM. It seems today means anytime within the next 24 hours as it is now 11:45 AM. The nurse wanders in occasionally and asks the same question: "Oh, are you still here?" This ought to be obvious, inasmuch as it seems I am the one to whom she directs the question. Then she leaves only to return 20 minutes later to ask the same question, which causes me to wonder if my physical presence is evident only to me. I am at the moment attached to a monitor, which allegedly displays some activity of my heart on a screen located in a chamber somewhere nearby. Is it possible that the signal on the screen has gone flat and perhaps I am, indeed, not here and that information has not yet reached me or the nurse who continues to be surprised by my presence?

My room is almost directly across the hallway from a series of small spaces occupied by numerous persons (mostly female) whose major activity seems to be talking, and as far as I can tell little of it is about me. Normally this wouldn't concern me except, given the current circumstances, I cannot escape the possibility that the absence of references to me is additional evidence that I am truly not here. Although I am aware of the destinies of oldsters leaving the hospital (other than home) I am unwilling at this moment to speculate about at which of these places I may be or to which I may be headed. >>>

I know that there are accountants among the conclaves across the hall. Given this day of electronic transfer of information and the extremely short lapse of time between a service received and the arrival of the bill in my mailbox, I could call Pat and ask if the hospital bill has arrived. But I am reluctant to do that and cause her to be alarmed about where I may be.

I am relieved. Pat just arrived. She reports that the hospital bill arrived in today's mail and she assumes that means I am free to go home. So I close down my laptop and go.

I leave physically restored but less certain about in whose hands my destiny rests.

APRIL 23

Meritocracy

With the possible exception of professors themselves, everybody harbors suspicions that we professors are a peculiar bunch. Four decades in academia observing professors has persuaded me that, as a group, we are more ordinary than most of us care to admit. We live and work, however, in a context where the rhetoric of distinction and elitism causes us to think of ourselves as anything but ordinary. Notions of excellence and brilliance are prattled about until everyone believes there actually is an objective scale of merit with the brightest on top and lesser lights on lower rungs all the way to the bottom. It is that kind of fantasy in which professors are free to indulge.

This scramble for recognition compromises the essential function of the educational enterprise. But that's not what this is about. It's about whether the notion that being number one has any lasting significance. Aspiring to be number one may be a flaw in the human soul and the striving thereto is more instinctive than we care to admit. At church last Sunday my thoughts turned to the meritocratic context of my professorial days. The minister talked of the debate of the disciples overheard by Jesus about which of them was the greatest, to which He replied, "If anyone wants to be first, he must be the very last and the servant of all." That's not easy. Number one isn't up for grabs in some arenas.

Merit doesn't matter in the exit lane.

APRIL 26

A Gene from Mom

This daily counting or recounting, as is often the case, begins with me seated before my iMac with a cup of coffee in one hand and the other on the keyboard. Works well for me as I have yet to learn to type with both hands. If I were compelled to give up either the keyboard or the coffee cup, I am fearful the keyboard would have to go. I learned of coffee from my Danish mother decades before the dawn of PCs or Starbucks.

In my earliest memories of my mother, her coffee cup is always in the picture. The ubiquitous coffee pot was always on the kitchen wood-burning stove. She made coffee first thing in the morning the old fashioned way by boiling coffee grounds in water to which a fresh egg has been added. The aroma seems to have been intoxicating. It has been said that olfactory memories are the most persistent. The only place one can find coffee like that is at a rural midwestern farm auction. This, incidentally, is the only pleasant feature of those events.

I used to say I was four years old before I realized that Mom's cup was not part of her hand. I don't do that anymore, fearful that it leaves the impression that I was a dumb kid. But her cup was always nearby. My earliest recollections of drinking coffee are sitting with Mom after school at the old oak dining-room table in the tiny log house we were crammed into the early days of my high school years. Those are cherished memories of intimate conversation with my mother, which became fewer after I went off to war. My former genetics students report that I justified the ever-present coffee cup on the lectern by suggesting that for everything, including a fondness for coffee, there is a gene. They would argue that my mother's genes had nothing to do with it—that it was a habit I had learned from her. They defined habit as behavior so deeply ingrained that it occurs without thought.

My mother lived ninety years and never gave much thought to the supposed liability of coffee consumption, but to her a cup of freshly brewed coffee was never thoughtless activity.

Either way, whether I learned or inherited a fondness for coffee from my mother, I am glad.

APRIL 27

Free Stuff

While very little in life is free, much is said about things that are. *The best things in life are free. No such thing as a free lunch. Free advice is worth the cost. Free puppies.* One cannot not notice the readiness with which folks queue up for giveaways, but seldom are free things free from consequences.

While it seemed less so then than it does in retrospect, we were poor folks during much of my boyhood years. I was born in the depth of the great depression. Concurrently, three years of drought in the dustbowl thirties devastated our crops. Ironically, our first post-drought crops were destroyed by a major hailstorm. Although our parents talked little about their financial struggles, we were poor indeed. To feed and clothe seven children was an unimaginable task, exacerbated by my proud Danish mother's intense reluctance to accept charity. To do so was an admission of personal weakness or failure, a flaw of character.

One source of tension between my parents was about what we kids unceremoniously referred to as *free stuff*. The New Deal—the government's assistance to desperate citizens included two programs that were especially ignominious to my mother.

Surplus commodities—governmental purchased food-stuff for which there was no market because people had no money—were distributed freely to needy people. My mother never traveled to town to receive *free goods* as we children callously called it. With humility and much to my mother's extreme and uncharacteristically vocal dismay, our father did.

Disquieted, perhaps, by parental spats about charity, we were seldom hungry. Mom's culinary improvisations with these discomfiting ingredients were extraordinary.

And then there was the matter of *free pants*. In the WPA (Work Progress Administration) women were hired to sew clothing that was available for in-need families. My mother, a competent seamstress by necessity, would rather have received the cloth and sewn the clothes herself—less injurious to her pride. But the program didn't work that way. My father also brought home trousers for my four brothers and me that (you guessed it!) we dubbed *free pants* I don't know about my brothers, but I wore my free pants with a new understanding of pride and humility.

Nobody knows whether the food one eats is free, but free pants? That's a dead giveaway.

APRIL 28

Senectitude

Young people have always been creatively inventing new ways with old words. These days, to expedite 'text messaging' portions of familiar words or words without vowels have crept into common parlance. Today I overheard two teenagers vociferously debating some difference of opinion. "Aw, come on, drop the 'tude, Dude," one of them said. Having spent much of my adult life with college kids, I have watched this minimization of words taking place. *Hanging out* has become *hanging* or simply *hang*. Attitude has become *tude*. There are others but to catalogue them is not the intent of this piece.

That overheard conversation fixed my mind on words that end with the suffix *-tude*. I was surprised at the number of such words that reside easily in my mental thesaurus. There are lots of them denoting, according to my etymological research, condition or state of being: attitude, solitude, rectitude, platitude, plenitude, certitude, similitude, altitude, magnitude, gratitude, aptitude, and beatitude. I was further amazed by how many of them aptly apply to elders. It might be said:

> There is certitude in their conclusions.

> They retire usually in rectitude, sometimes in solitude, but rarely in plenitude.

> They openly express gratitude for the magnitude of their good fortunes.

> In reference to the good old days, they resort to platitudes.
>
> Their attitudes are clear; their aptitudes become less so.
>
> Their visages are a study in similitude.

I stumbled onto a little used one of these *-tude* words when perusing a dictionary of synonyms. I was looking to enlarge my repertoire of words that denote aging—other than senile, senility, and senescence (words that I find hurtful). The word is *senectitude*, defined as the condition of being old.

Can it be said that anyone actually enjoys senectitude?

APRIL 30

By Any Other Name

My name is Howard. I have never totally reconciled with the moniker. My parents named me during a bit of duress. The Dictionary of Proper Names defines Howard as *ward or keeper of the hall* or janitor in contemporary jargon. I have no ill will or feeling of condescension toward janitors. I worked competently as a custodian for six years while in college. It has been said that one becomes what one is named. That seems to have happened to me, but not in the way the dictionary implies.

In the continuing erosion of classroom formality, addressing professors by their first names became acceptable classroom protocol. This works well for profs named Bob or Bill or some other harmless tag that can't be made to carry an innuendo. But my name is Howard. And despite the protocol, there was something about Howard that seemed to cause my students to be apologetic for calling me that. Never in forty years in the profession did a student address me by my given name. Perhaps they recognized that having been named Howard is something one never gets over and they wished not to call attention to that.

Howard was not my folks' first choice. They intended to name their first male child Hans, the name of both my Danish and Norwegian grandfathers. What they didn't know was there would be two of us and they had to choose two names. They could have named us both Hans. There is no law precluding that. >>>

What they did instead was retain the first letter of Hans and select names from a list that begin with the letter H. It doesn't require literary genius to know that the list of names beginning with H is not prime nomenclature. What healthy kid wants to answer to Hubert, or Henry, or Humphrey, or Hugh, or Hector, or Herman, or Helmut? I suppose I should be grateful that the list included Harold and Howard—the least unacceptable in that index—because that's what they decided to name us.

Unable to decide which of the two of us should be named Howard, they asked my Danish grandfather Hans, who had come to assess this twin phenomenon. "That one looks like a professor—call him Howard," he said pointing to me. "Name the other one Harold. He looks like a politician." Harold did become a politician, a good one. He had a talent for the impossible.

I marvel at Granddad's premonition.

May

MAY 5
Files

"Don't leave the decisions to us," our daughters announced upon surveying our rather extensive library of files, the accumulation of two professional careers. Sorting through the accretion is a task that my proclivity to procrastinate too readily forestalls. It requires real intention to subdue the inertia and get to it. Some of it is still good reading (too prized for the wastebasket and reassigned to the files) like this e-mail note sent to grandson Jordan while he was deployed to Iraq. The files diminish slowly.

> Hey Jordan,
>
> The past several days there has been constant TV coverage of Ronald Reagan's State funeral with all the tribute, symbolism, pomp, and ceremony of which the country is capable. I am sure all of this has been shown on the Armed Forces outlets and that you may have seen some of it. I watched this all with considerable interest, no little fascination, and at times with some disquiet.
>
> I was most impressed with the military as they went about their ceremonial assignments. The soldiers, airmen, sailors, and marines performed their ceremonial assignments with style and dignity, with precision and professionalism, some of which seemed physically demanding. I found myself searching the faces of those tall, strong, handsome soldiers looking for you. >>>

I imagined you as the tall, dignified, gentle sergeant who escorted Mrs. Reagan, as a drummer in the Army Band, or standing guard in the capitol rotunda, escorting the caisson along Pennsylvania Avenue, singing with the Air Force Singing Sergeants, or flying in the Missing Man formation. (I tried imagining myself in one of those roles, but it didn't work—there are no short guys chosen for up-front duty.) I found it remarkable that all those guys were generally good looking chaps. There is a sense in which all soldiers by virtue of their uniforms are handsome guys. And then there are also, as you and I know, guys who are handsome by virtue of a good gene pool.

With great objectivity,

Granddad

MAY 6

Out of Nowhere

One day in a small North Dakota town next to nowhere a little girl was born. Today the little girl, now grown older, lives a lot closer to somewhere and to everybody. Her journey has taken her to Chicago, Minneapolis, Los Angles, Denver, Seattle, London, and Copenhagen, places most consider to be somewhere of significance. But it is not those places that account for the beauty and grace of the woman who just finished eighty treks around the sun.

That distinction belongs to the folks of that small North Dakota town next to nowhere. Folks who would be omitted as nobodies from the world's lists of somebodies, who took her in, nurtured her body, soul, and mind. They taught her love, grace, and faith—lessons that never failed her.

She moved through other places never far from nowhere—Bird Island, Braham, Benge, Randolph, Wishek, Laramie, and Spokane. But not without notice. Those places, little known to all but those who have been there, are better for her having been there. How do I know? Sixty years ago I met her in one of those out-of-the-way places, and it has been my incredible good fortune to have moved with her to all places large and small and watch with pride and wonder at her persistent display of talent, beauty, love, and amazing grace.

Has it not been asked before: Can anything good come out of places next to nowhere?

MAY 7

A Birthday

> PREAMBLE: The text of the Psalmist's admonition to consider one's days reads literally *Number your days*. The authority of Holy Script notwithstanding, I submit that one's days are seldom exclusively one's own. Some days are inherently noteworthy because of momentous events on those days in some previous annual procession of days. These are days which count and have been counted and recounted. These days can never be my days alone, days on which my significance recedes in the presence of those given to me to cherish. I will be especially attentive to these days as they arise in this numbering of days. I am talking birthdays here, and today was Pat's birthday.

Pat and I traveled to Minnesota to attend the production of The Lion King. Serendipitously, we secured tickets for the performance on this day, the anniversary of Pat's birth. I know of no one more unabashedly enthusiastic about good professional theatre. I indulge myself with the notion that this—a fitting birthday present—was all my idea.

We attended the production with Suzanne and Terry who represent our clan in the great Twin City metropolis, renowned for its theatrical sophistication. The extent to which aging Norwegians can be that way, I was enchanted with the show. The puppetry, choreography, and scenic design were captivating. I marveled at the creativity both in conception and production manifested on the stage. But I digress.

Although I enjoyed the show immensely, this is not about good theatre. It's about Pat who knows good theatre. I have observed with fascination (and pride) the manner in which she has exploited her natural talent, exquisite voice, and dedicated study to make printed words come alive. Not only has she an uncanny ability to imagine how words should be spoken to reveal their meaning but how to speak them so as to conjure those images in the minds of audiences. She excelled in coaching wanna-be student actors in honing their oral reading skills.

I have what I believe to be a normal adult attention span, but I confess to allowing my mind to wander during staged activities—symphonic, operatic, or theatrical—and to ponder with profound gratitude my good fortune of having been tutored in the finer aspects of life by a true artist born on this day.

It was Pat's birthday, but the gift was mine.

MAY 7
Birthday Thoughts

There are, I believe, two assumptions that linger near the surface of our thoughts as we acknowledge and celebrate a birthday. There are emotions that tug in opposite directions. The same day we call birthday marks both end and beginning—the close of a year and the start of another, gratitude and hope, thanksgiving and expectation.

When our years move into the upper reaches of our biblical allotment, both the gratitude and hope become more intense. While reckoning with reality, we live on in expectation more profoundly aware of God's grace in these accumulated years and a keener alertness for new reasons to praise Him.

All of this is proem to the impact of birthdays on the numbering of our days urged by the ancient poet. Birthdays, inherently numbered, are days that count, that is, count for something. Today is Pat's birthday and few of the days in my accrual of days count for much apart from her presence in them. Her birthday conjures countless days of joy and hope and the anticipation of good times yet to count.

Eighty-two and counting.

May 7, 2008

MAY 8
Off the Hook

Ever wonder when you first encountered or learned a word and added it to your personal *worterbuch*? My fascination with words often draws me into a bit of idle word processing. Not in the manner of arranging words via computer word-processing programs, but cerebral rumination about words, meanings, and my introduction to them. It is difficult to precisely determine when certain words become fixed in one's mental thesaurus, but reminders of those occasions surface in my thoughts more frequently now that retirement has cleared the background noise of the brain's busyness with activity essential to making a living. I believe that some words attain a special fondness (or aversion) in one's hierarchy of favorite words. For reasons I have not attempted to understand until now, I seldom use the word *exempt*.

Recently when reviewing tax returns with our tax consultant, the notion of exemptions emerged. Tax exemptions, that is, with an attending sense of relief. Exemptions in conversations about taxes invariably conjure a sense of good fortune. Today after an extensive exam my doctor said, "You seem to be exempt from many of the exigencies of aging." That's an exemption I can live with.

There was a period in my lifetime when the word *exempt* was thrust into the collective thinking of the populace. It was wartime. Young men were subject to conscription into military service. Exemption from the call was as varied as were the young men coming of age (18 years). To some it was relief. They were off the hook. For others their wish to serve was thwarted or delayed. Unfortunately, exemption was stigmatic. Society became suspicious of the loyalty of apparently healthy young men among the civilian population.

From our extended family there were nine first cousins who volunteered, including brother Dick and me. "No draft dodgers in our family," my most zealously patriotic aunt would say. That was especially hurtful to my twin brother Harold who, unfortunately due to an enlarged and impaired heart, was ignominiously classified 4F by the draft board. Several 'patriots' careless enough to suggest that he had dodged the bullet or was off the hook found themselves on their backs looking at stars. He had a vicious left hook.

Harold lived with distinction; gained the respect of friends by the hundreds who crowded his untimely memorial service. Sadly he never overcame the cause of his exemption from military service in the Great War. His big heart served his fellow humans well, but it failed to exempt him from the consequences of aging, as my doctor would say.

That is an exemption I had cherished for both of us.

MAY 9

Brothers Five

Today I went to visit with Ray, the youngest and only survivor of my four brothers. "I am going to live to be ninety," he had promised the last time we had been together, which is infrequent because we live 1,500 miles apart. It seemed as if he was making a promise with the expectation that asserting the aspiration would assure the goal. Secretly, while I marveled at the promise, I thought given his recent health challenges the expectation was ambitious, if not a bit audacious.

Today, however, as we chatted it became apparent that he had abandoned that ambition and had become resigned to the realities of aging. We talked briefly about our departed brothers and the bonus days that he and I have been awarded. I am quite sure that we both silently wondered, considering health and distance, whether this might be our final face-to-face conversation.

As we drove home I reviewed, as elderly thinkers are wont to do, memories of the brothers five and composed this simple but sobering bit of poetry:

Five brothers standing at the door
One walked through
And then there were four.

Four brothers walking by the sea
One stepped in
And then there were three.   >>>

Three brothers sitting in the pew
One stood to leave
And then there were two.

Two brothers resting in the sun
One went to sleep
And then there was one.

One brother now walks alone
Pondering the end of this brief poem.

Only Almighty God knows whether Ray or I
will sign this poem.

MAY 10

Empty Words

The popular newsman, Walter Cronkite, closed his newscasts with the declaration: *And that's the way it is.* One would think the way things are would be obvious to anyone paying attention. But of all places one might expect that to be true, it is anything but obvious. It is in the arena of words where the way things are is seldom as obvious as they could be.

A major perquisite of retirement is time and opportunity to read. Consequently, my excursions into words have extended into areas vastly more varied than the arena to which I was constrained by professional demands. I wander freely in the realms of fiction, poetry, philosophy, theology, science, politics, and history. It seems that what many former historians wrote was not the way it was. Currently the stories once told about Washington, Franklin, and Lincoln are said to have missed major aspects of the way it was and apparently history needs rewriting.

That's OK, I suppose. It gives scholars something to do and people like me something to read and fret about. For example, what on earth difference does it make whether Washington smiled a lot or never smiled at all? Except for an accolade in the bio of the writer and a few dollars in the coffers of bookmakers, that bit of nonsense contributes little to the well being of the masses.

But I must move on lest I stumble into the pit I am digging for others. (The prophet wrote, *Beware of the trap you dig for others, lest you fall therein.*) Much of scholarly writing is fraught with unnecessary words. Words as a means of telling it like it is (or was) have become an end in themselves. And the manipulation of words, no matter how ingenious, frequently obscures the way it is (or was). To get to the way it is becomes tedious. One wonders how those who perpetrate the notion that many words are good missed the warning of the ancient wise man of Ecclesiastes who wrote, *The more words one uses, the greater the emptiness of it all, and where is the profit in that?*

But that is the way it has become.

MAY 11

Statistical Disquiet

At the restaurant this evening I saw a tall, slender, somewhat gnarled, white-haired gentleman, whom I judged to be about my age. I watched surreptitiously as he stiffly extracted himself from the booth and, bent ever so slightly, walked by. He is one of us, my mind insisted. Not primarily one of us eighty-something guys, but one of the group that Tom Brokaw dubbed (generously, I think) The Greatest Generation. My intuition was right. On the back of his jacket was the inscription: Submarine Veterans of WWII.

There was dissonance in this picture. He was, at his age, still a tall man. How ever did he make his way about the constricted passages of the submarines of that era, I thought. Did he have stories to tell and to whom he did tell them, I wondered. Did he think of himself as one of the great ones?

"What are you thinking about?" Pat asked, as she often does when it becomes apparent that my mind is chasing an idea.

What emotional contentment or comfort am I entitled to because I, like the gent who just walked by, happened to be part of a particular subset of guys who were born in the 1920s? Did my twin brother miss greatness because an unfortunate physical limitation precluded military service? I am more apt to think greatness when reminiscing about him than when I think about my military capers.

The event that drew us 'great guys' apart from the rest of the generation has faded into memory. The most personally disturbing aspect of the current rhetoric about it is the statistical observation that is invariably appended to references to "the greatest generation." We are dying at the rate of 1,000 a day.

What is so great about that?

MAY 12

Program Notes

The expression downsizing, popular the last few decades to denote reduction in personnel or inventories, is an appropriate description of the activities of oldsters getting their affairs in order in preparation for a move to a smaller residence or other destinations. Getting rid of a life-long accumulation of personal stuff—books, photos, letters, documents, and papers—can be emotionally strenuous. Decisions about the tangible stuff like the car, house, furniture, and bank account may be left for later generations to ponder.

This downsizing caper may consume a lot of time depending on one's pack-rat proclivities, but oldsters usually have ample time for other than routine daily chores. Some amusing and pleasant surprises emerge as one sifts through a trove of stuff set aside for future consideration. Pat and her sisters were amused to discover their mother had saved every Valentine candy box she had received from students during four decades of teaching.

My cache of memorabilia has been reduced to written or printed materials saved originally for reasons that often no longer exist. Much of it now appears to have been motivated mostly by vanity. Not unlike most wanna-be scholars, I confess seeing my name in print has always given me a private sense of worth (especially following the words, *Pay to the order of*).

Sorting my papers one final time, I found an assortment of printed programs on which my name appears. I think I saved them to remind me and whoever may notice that I was momentarily a person of consequence. My favorite among these souvenirs is a program for the Commencement activities at Migh College several years ago. The agenda announced that I was chosen by the students to present the Baccalaureate sermon, which I had entitled MOLECULAR MORALITY. The senior student whose task it was to present me to the assembled graduates and their parents, without explanation, introduced me as BIOLOGIAN IN RESIDENCE, a bit of irony about a biologist gone to preaching.

A letter from an offended English major alumnus, a real preacher, sternly chastised me for my showy oxymoronic title and incongruent professional designation. His note applauded the title of the popular and venerable English professor's commencement address.

He spoke eloquently about AN ALLIGATOR ALLEGORY.

MAY 13

Symphonic Subtlety

We went to the symphony last evening. I was a tad resistant. It was the height of the NBA championship play-offs, but friends unable to attend the last concert of the season generously offered us their tickets. Bob wanted to watch the game. Inasmuch as some basketball contests are as dull as some lengthy, raucous, dissonant symphonic concerts, the decision was sixes (my daughter's shorthand for six of one or a half dozen of another). I lost the coin toss and we went to the symphony.

The program was unusually varied, I thought. There were chorale voices and ballet dancers. There was Strauss, Janacek, Verdi, Saint-Saëns and Tchaikovsky. My musical sophistication is not a total wash. I recognized Saint-Saëns and Tchaikovsky. It was the other stuff that allowed my mind to stray.

My musing conjured analogies between the appoggiaturas on the stage and the antics on, let's say, a football field. There is the coach (conductor), the quarterback (concertmaster), the line backers (cellists), the offensive line (brass), the defensive backs (bassoon and contrabass)—heavy but mobile, the cheerleaders (ballerinas). Musical jargon has even crept into the comments of athletes, The quarterback being interviewed at halftime intermission confesses that he hadn't orchestrated very well before the intermission. >>>

The analogizing grew a bit wearisome and I began to wonder whether I was into analogy, allegory, metaphor, or simile. I recall saying to my high school English teacher, "Analogy, allegory, metaphor, simile—whatever." It was then she, not very subtly, introduced me to the notion of subtlety.

Subtlety is wherever you find it.

MAY 14

Divine Diversion

Yesterday Pat and I traveled 90 miles to join a community of cattle ranchers and wheat growers and their extended families to attend the Centennial Year celebration of their small town. When we made our first trip there 37 years ago, it was to embark on a delightful journey that continues still.

About the time I had mastered the practices and protocols of the professoriate, I received an ironic and unexpected invitation from a small congregation there to become their pastor. The request was not without credibility. We had been guests of the congregation on several occasions and were already acquainted with these folks. They were my kind of people in whose presence I could revisit my early fantasies about farming, which I had abandoned at the age of 26 to go to college—ironically to become a preacher.

But I had become instead a card-carrying, reductionist, biology professor, the species about whom many church-goers are most suspicious. I was comfortable spending my days learning about and marveling at the awesome cellular and molecular intricacies of living matter.

Moreover, I was untrained in the art of preaching, of visiting the ill, eulogizing the departed, comforting the saddened, marrying the young, cautioning the wayward, and affirming the kind deeds and good will of the faithful. None of which are assignments on the job description of a molecular biology professor. It seemed presumptuous of me to acquire these skills at their expense, so I declined the call with the provision that I would fill the role until they could find a person truly prepared for the task.

Seven years later they had long abandoned their search. I had become their preacher, searching with them the mysterious intangibles of living souls. They taught me well. I was quick to acknowledge what they did for me. Their embrace, encouragement, hospitality, affirmation, and gracious goodwill enriched my professional and personal well being beyond all expectation. Seldom did they seem impressed or intimidated by my professorial credentials. Not only did they faithfully listen to my sermons, they invited me to help (or to believe I was helping) with their ranching activities. I operated their harvest machinery, worked the round-up and other cattle chores, assisted with building projects, fought wildfires, and mended fences.

All of this at the expense, my professional colleagues would say, of my reputation in the society of professional biologists. Summers and weekends, they warned me, were for immersing oneself in the minutiae and extending the margins of one's ideological niche.

Naïvely, I suppose, but seldom did I worry about my professional reputation as we traveled by the wheat fields and ranch land on my way to proclaim biblical truths at the little church.

The little church and its people beckon still.

MAY 16

My Donkey

One often hears elderly folks deprecated for their predisposition to dwell in the past. Aware of that stereotype, alert ancients like me limit our conversations to recent activities, which in many instances aren't nearly as exciting nor as significant as events of earlier times. Like the time I almost shot my brother. Actually, one gets few chances to tell about an occasion like that and should use great care in exploiting the opportunities, because once you have told the story it becomes old news. Young people are indifferent to news, especially old news. "Oh, Granddad," the grandkids say, "You told that story yesterday." Makes one wonder what, if anything, is worth repeating. Someday I will tell you about that day. It wasn't my fault.

Like most oldsters, I find myself saying *in retrospect* with increasing frequency. My dictionary defines retrospection as the remembering of past events, which incidentally I think is a healthy thing for an octogenarian mind to do. Because the ratio of past to future shifts to the past, we live in retrospection. I have no reason to think that my mental processes differ much from others my age, except I may be a bit more reticent to repeat my reminisces and risk becoming predictable.

Looking back came early for me. My battle station was the tail gunner position in the B-17 bomber my buddies and I flew on sorties over major European cities. One might say I rode backwards through the battles. By the time the bombs reached the ground the plane had traveled far beyond the target and I was in the best position to assess the consequences.

Last evening I read a comment by one of my favorite theologians, now 90 years old. He told of an ancient Chinese philosopher who was asked why he was riding his donkey facing backwards. *We live life looking forward. We understand life looking backward,* he said. Understanding memorable moments of one's past necessitates no little looking back. It is good for both mind and soul. But not unlike the ride in the back seat of a bomber, it's lonely.

Most young folks are too busy looking ahead to have time to ride on my donkey looking back.

MAY 17

The Willow Switch

It was Mother's Day. The minister, a woman, spoke of mothers and grace. My mind chased ahead of the speaker and rested on memories of my mother and her counsel on the consequences of wrongdoing.

A friend from a neighboring farm functioned on the margins of right and wrong, especially when he was out of the reach of his parents, that is, when he was allowed to roam Main Street while his parents were attending to the weekly shopping. He had begun to indulge in minor shoplifting. On one occasion he demonstrated the ease with which he could pocket a handful of candy from the open displays at the local Five & Dime store. Later, I naively demonstrated the technique to my twin brother. I snitched a single jelly-bean. To my dismay Harold announced he was going to 'tell.'

My mother's religious instruction was clear. The distinctions between rascally pranks, naughtiness, and sin were precise. Swiping jellybeans from a sibling's stash was naughty, but shoplifting even a single jellybean was sin. Harold knew that and used his knowledge to blackmail me to do his assigned chores. For the next two weeks, laden with guilt, I quietly did his chores (and mine).

Mom's corrective techniques were effective. She had five boys to keep off the road to perdition. A couple of swipes with the willow switch were reserved for the worst offenses. >>>

Stealing even a single jellybean was not simple naughtiness. It was sinful. Wearied with guilt and double-duty chores, I confessed my transgression and pled forgiveness. My mother had been expecting me.

Not only did I avoid the willow switch, I learned of grace.

MAY 20

Decades

While most folks don't think all that much about it, octogenarians are, in fact, in the ninth decade of their lives and have attained an age when life is more conveniently thought about in decades.

I have no data except my own recollections, but I suspect that's what oldsters reminiscing about the past are inclined to do—think in larger chunks like decades. It's a more economical use of one's reminiscentory energy. (I know reminiscentory is not a word, but it should be.) Consider the different scenarios conjured by a year in the life of Billy the Kid or Stephen Foster's Old Black Joe. All of this is a proem to thoughts about reviewing one's past.

Pat and I still occasionally ease back into main-stream traffic and travel across the states by automobile. Except in eastern Montana where the scenery becomes a bit monotonous, nature's varied beauty is best honored by wonder and silence and a lot of chatter isn't necessary. In eastern Montana, however, where the sky is big and the horizon is far away we sometimes break into conversation. Pat's tolerance of silence is not as refined as mine. One exercise we engage in (to manage the quiet and pass the time) is to reminisce with some nostalgia about other roads we have traveled.

"Looking back," Pat asks, "what decade of our sojourn (she probably wouldn't say sojourn—that's my word) do you think back on with the fondest memories?" Our lives now, it seems, divide easily into distinct decades. The drought and depression of the dirty thirties. High school, war, courtship in the fighting forties. Farming, new car, new direction in the flamboyant fifties. By now we cross the line into North Dakota and the conversation slows, as does the speed limit.

The decades go on. We, like all of our 80-something friends, are finding our way in the ninth decade. Chances that we will look back at this decade from any distance aren't all that good.

P.S. It's been a great trip, but I like the romantic 40's best.

MAY 25

Moved by Time

All humans have a sense of the passing of time. This sense, called *time awareness* by one of my favorite biologists, is what he insisted is our *ultimate concern*. Einstein taught us that time is truly the fourth dimension of our existence. The spatial aspects of our everyday experience tend to stay put. Space tends to stay in place, but time seems to move. Time passes with us, it seems. However, another thinker under whose tutelage I sat was wont to say, "Time is—we march on."

When we think of or conjure images of people we know it is usually in the context of place. But it is not space that defines or changes us as much as it is time. This old house has been the space in which we, Pat and I, have moved about individually and together for 25 years. This space (the round house, as we call it) has changed us little, but not so the time of 25 years in this space.

The space has been delightful, comfortable, and constant. The stuff of time is change and challenge—physically, spiritually, mentally. We grow, regress, succeed, conquer, believe and hope. We reckon with reality and the limits of longevity in the context of time, not so with space.

Time is as real as space, but it's time that does its thing with us.

MAY 28

Remembering

Today is the start of the annual Memorial Day celebration, made bigger in recent years by events at the WW II Memorial in Washington. The media hype and the critique of the memorial sort of jerk me around. I think I agree with the critics about the design. It tries to say too much. Something simpler and more subtle, I think, would honor the vets with the dignity these guys deserve at this time in their lives.

I also agree that it should have happened long ago when many more of the vets could have experienced it. I learned last night that of the 16,000,000 men honored by the monument only 3,000,000 remain alive. I have fantasized about being there with those old guys some Memorial weekend, but in contrast to most of the stories being told (perhaps for the first time) by the old guys shown on TV, my story would be a rather minor footnote.

As the definitions of *veteran* and *war* become more uncertain, it will become more difficult to design much less find room for meaningful memorials. One reads in history about "the hundred-year war" or "the thirty-year war." I am afraid we (contemporary humankind) too have embarked on a very long conflict. How will anyone know when it's over and will anyone be left to build the memorial? I suppose as long as humans exist there will be wars. And as long as there are wars there will be memorials in remembrance of those who fought the battles. But who wants to remember? I sense the old guys gathering at this latest memorial would rather forget.

Does it still matter?

MAY 29

You Don't Say!

It has been said by pundits, who ponder such things, that the human tendency to categorize objects, events, or persons has significant survival value. It allows us, they say, to cope with the complexity of nature and chaos of existence. Primitive peoples' survival certainly was enhanced by a priori suspicions of good and bad guys.

I think our proclivity to classify leads to stereotyping, a kind of short-cut thinking. Along with the boxes in which we instinctively place people there is an automatic, unthinking response, which enables us to dismiss individuals because of our preconceived notions about *people like that.*

On the other hand, things, events and people tend naturally to fall into boxes. I have been thinking about a recent participation in a discussion with a randomly chosen group, some of whom I knew and others whom I didn't. Group palaver is an all too common activity among professors. I don't do much of that anymore.

I like to believe I am above stereotyping but as this session progressed I realized I had relapsed into old habits. A professor in the group was affirming that, of all people, professors are most likely to live up to their stereotypic expectations. One can always count on professors to talk too much.

Others in the group fell readily into my store of people boxes, that is, persons who had only one thing to say and said it often; persons who had nothing to say and did the same;

persons who keep talking while thinking of something to say. And then there were the quiet ones.

I am most curious about the silent ones. They may be wise enough to know that when one has nothing to say it is best not to say it. There is merit, I submit, in avoiding the temptation to keep talking until one has thought of something to say. But that risks missing one's turn. I didn't say much. Too old or too wise, I know not which.

I have heard it said that it is better to remain silent and appear a fool than to speak and remove all doubt. The writer of the Old Testament Proverbs declares, *Even a fool is thought wise if he keeps silent, and discerning if he holds his tongue.* Proverbs 17:28

Quiet people aren't the only ones who don't say much.

MAY 31

For Beth on Memorial Day

Today is Memorial Day—a day designated especially for remembering. My first recollections of Memorial Day are about going to the cemetery as a child to beautify gravesites. At that time the day set aside for remembering was called Decoration Day. The very act of being at the tombstone of a significant person would, I suspect, evoke memories sad as well as pleasant. But why wait until a gravestone appears? I think remembering ought to be an ongoing practice—moments when the thoughts of another person flicker in one's mental imagery and are free to linger.

I am proposing a Memorable Day's Day not limited to one day per annum. Rather, days when one intentionally reviews and enlarges one's inventory of memorable days with persons of consequence. I will initiate the proposal by listing memorable days that inhabit my memories of you, though not in chronological sequence or prominence.

Memorable Days with Beth Ann: told by birth nurse you had the expected number of toes and fingers; seeing through the nursery window that your last name was misspelled; looking for a lost little girl sleeping in the closet; dam trips with Rich and Jinny; running the gravel roads at Chattaroy; discussing the expediency of rag-tied curls on the way to Jr. High; watching you leave on your first solo in the Saab; eating sweet corn at Uncle Milton's place; framing walls of the round house; watching your Bethel acting

73

debut; trips to the animal house at U of W; staying in our travel trailer at the Clinesmith ranch; your encounter with the Woodway Park bulldogs; running the paved roads at Indian Trail; going to church at Trinity Baptist; dining on rabbit at Lucille Allert's place; hauling ice storm debris; driving to college in the Honda CVCC; walking the aisle at Bethlehem Baptist. There's more, much more, but you get the idea.

Each Memorable Day's Day, I enlarge the list.

F.o.B.*

---

*Father of Beth

June

JUNE 1

Throwaway Days

The dean of students at Migh College was a craggy, unsophisticated math teacher. His counseling of confused and troubled students was the same for all who sought help. "Lets pray about it," he would say. He believed that the source of all internal disquiet resulted from spiritual inadequacy. While it may be that some disquiet accrues from uncertainty about matters of spirit, it is also true that the deep, personal, mental turmoil and confusion about what's going on in one's head during a bout of depression may be spiritual in that it seems illogical, disconnected, mysterious, and defies understanding. Yet the disquiet is profoundly real. I know. I have been there.

This mental derailment causes one to feel or think about oneself (or just as often to not feel or think at all) in ways that are painful, defeating, and paralyzing. I don't intend to imply that prayer doesn't matter or lessen the distress. While there is little salvageable in a day lived in the mire of depression, life is too precious to count some days as throwaway days.

The enemies with whom the Psalmist David constantly battled and from whom he petitioned for release were not only warring neighbors but internal demons that at one time or another plague all of God's people. Here is some of what he wrote: *I waited patiently for the Lord and He inclined unto me and heard my cry. He brought me up also out of a horrible pit, out of the miry clay, and set my feet upon a rock and established my goings. And He put a new song in my heart, even praise unto our God.* >>>

77

Now from the sublime to the ridiculous. You have seen the TV ad asserting: "There are things that money can't buy. For everything else there's MasterCard." In this context the ad might be: "There are some things pills can fix. For everything else there is prayer!"

Maybe old Dean Butler was right.

JUNE 2

A Perfect Day

Somewhere along the way in my progression of days, probably during an excursion into poetry in high school, I was exposed to these lines by James Russell Lowell.

> *What is so rare as a day in June?*
> *Then, if ever, come perfect days.*

Why these lines stand out in my memory, while others perhaps equally mesmeric are long gone, I can't know. I suspect some disquiet about the notion of a perfect day keeps it there.

In this counting or recounting of days proposed by Holy Script I have discovered, recovered, or uncovered some very good days. And while I haven't necessarily been on the lookout for a perfect day, I have become convinced that days inhabited by an imperfect guy like me will never attain perfection. That is, "a perfect day" is an empty category, the poet's words notwithstanding.

None of this is an indictment on life, especially not on my days. In my reflections on living I find no reason not to be extremely glad about the journey. June is nice and especially in our corner of the country. If one were in search of a perfect day, June would be a wise time to begin.

If the poem is, as often is the case, meant to be analogous with life, then spring quivering with life affords us the best hope of perfection and we oldsters may do well to forget it. A perfect day in December would indeed be rare. >>>

Have I quit looking? While it's not something I can know with certainty, I harbor the strong belief that there does indeed lie ahead that rare, perfect day.

That's the premise of my counting.

JUNE 4

Peripheral Perceptions

One aspect of these ninth decade days that not only surprises but also intrigues me is the extent to which we oldsters become observers at the edges of functioning society. Obviously the effect of that varies extensively depending on individual expectations and emotional needs. It may be devastating to one used to the attention of center stage or great relief to one grown weary of the limelight. I assume there are scholars studying the psychological distress of people disquieted by the shove to the sidelines. After all, sociologists need something to do to keep them out of the way. But I digress.

This is about what, I submit, is one subtle benefit of the sideline seats. They afford us old-timers a delightful or troubling change in perspective—an opportunity to see, in many cases, why things didn't work, things that got in the way, things one missed up close.

Last Sunday I observed (from balcony seats) the Commencement exercises of my professorial alma mater. I was there to affirm the graduation of granddaughter Abbie. Fifteen years had passed since last I participated in the pomposity of one of these affairs. Sunday's event didn't vary significantly from similar events in which I willingly, maybe even enthusiastically, participated during thirty-five professional years.

I am uncertain whether due to newfound objectivity or renewed cynicism, I watched the proceedings with massive dissonance. The event seemed awash in hubris, pretense, and displays of meritocratic arrogance. I could not admit at the moment that I had ever done that. I must have, however. A former student, now a professor, was there proudly wearing the academic regalia I gave him when I took down my shingle.

I wonder what else watching the parade from the sidelines will reveal.

JUNE 5

Solemnity

Student legend identifies me as the prof who never smiled before the last day of the semester. I insist that is more fable than fact, but will acknowledge I am unable to produce a genuine smile upon request, much less on command. I never rebuked a student for laughing or smiling, but in jest I occasionally displayed a sign on my office door, which read THANKS FOR NOT SMILING. Student and public reaction to my slogan caused me to smile on occasion. It was during the time when NO SMOKING signs were common and many hurrying by read it that way. I thought it was funny, but in the context of the legend many students seemed perplexed.

My classroom confabulations were seldom devoid of humor. Occasionally an alert student would be amused by a bit of wit and burst into laughter while many of the others, too busy learning, would only wonder what had happened. I often reminded students that, if while lecturing I stopped talking and looked up expectantly, I had either asked a question or told a joke. If it was the latter, what I had just said wouldn't be on the exam and in spite of my solemn countenance it was OK to laugh.

But the nuances of my sign did occur to some, which led to pleasant, sometimes amusing conversations about why I put the sign there. Was I serious or what were the consequences should they be amused at some bit of humor in the chit-chat. You see — managing professors is an essential skill all students should learn.

I found the sign amongst some memorabilia I was sorting recently. The discovery reminded me of a conversation with a student about where I got the sign. I told him I stole it from the old Scandinavian Lutheran church where I first learned about matters of faith and worship protocols from stoic Norwegian immigrants. The sign, unnecessary there, would not have been out of place. But in some contemporary places of worship it might be especially appropriate.

I would like to believe God is pleased with smiling faces and bouncing bodies singing Joy to the World. But I wonder whether He might prefer a bit of physical restraint and worshipful solemnity when we sing When I Survey the Wondrous Cross.

I think I am going to bring my sign to church next Sunday.

JUNE 12

Hidden Talent

Ever been surprised by the realization that you have witnessed someone working in a role that didn't fit your stereotypic expectations? Today in a parking lot I watched a 110-pound young woman climb into a monster four-wheel-drive pickup. Noticing my look of incredulity, she informed me that her at-work-rig was a gigantic hook & ladder firetruck.

We expect football linemen to be huge guys and basketball players to be tall. All other things being equal a 300-pound tackle beats a 185-pound little guy. Same thing is true of the 7-foot center and a 6-foot dwarf. The advantages of such physical attributes are obvious. Conversely, there seems to be no need for top-rung sopranos or tenors to be as girthy as they tend to become. There was a time when film stars had to be far-above-the-mean beautiful or handsome, but apparently we have learned that acting skills are just as probable in folks with modest physiognomy.

Still we tend to be surprised when we encounter scrawny little men with booming bass voices or large, smiley hunks tenderly caring for babies in the hospital. I heard a poet once who seemed to me to be more burly than a poet needed to be. I knew of a bigger-than-most football player with amazing artistry in needlework.

One needs only to watch a symphonic orchestra in performance to observe that God packs the gifts he bestows in unlikely boxes. Or sit in on a meeting of professors attempting to do the faculty's business. I have, and I have learned that profound wisdom can issue forth from the least prestigious first-year instructor as readily as from the popular, prominent, professorial star.

Matching the intellectual and verbal skills with the embodiment of the scholarly practitioners was a delightful diversion from the tedium of many such confabulations. There was the scientist of substandard stature but huge in insight; the quite homely poet elegantly beautiful in spirit; the person erudite in demeanor but inane in dialogue. Others were simple in countenance but profound in discourse; sartorially splendid but logically sloppy; articulate but awfully addicted to alliteration.

Professors aren't all portraits of perfection or profundity.

JUNE 15

Eating Crow

Mother Goose rhymes surface frequently in my musings these days. Most folks my age will remember the Mother Goose poem that included the line: *Four and twenty blackbirds baked in a pie.* The idea of meat pie was not foreign to folks in our rural neighborhood. Chicken pot pie was served often at our family supper table. It was rumored that families of ethnic heritages other than ours exploited the ubiquitous abundance of sparrows and served an occasional sparrow pie. While I was never confronted with the delicacy, I tended to believe that some families did indeed prepare the dish. Our family did harvest, roast, and serve young pigeons that hatched among the rafters of our haymow. Only later when grown and worldly did I realize that we had dined on a big city delicacy known as squab.

Our regular avian cuisine included chicken, duck, turkey, goose and, when we became old enough to handle our family shotgun, seasonal fowl like pheasants, quail, wild ducks and geese, all deliciously prepared in the wood-fired kitchen range by our Danish mother. But never did we eat blackbirds, which I remember from childhood poetry were first served to royalty. It wasn't, however, because I didn't try.

During my boyhood we lived in a very small log house about 300 yards from Minnesota's Chippewa River. It was our favorite place to swim, fish, hunt and just stroll among the tall deciduous trees that grew along the banks. I often wandered there alone at dusk, a soothing mystical experience. A clump of densely spaced poplar trees at a bend in the river served as a rookery for the regional ravens—big, black, noisy birds that in my youthful imagination might well have been like those served to the king. In fact, when I was younger I asked an older cousin what he was going to do with a mess of crows he had shot. "Oh," he said nonchalantly, "probably make a pie."

I took my shotgun one evening and the one unexpended shotgun shell left over from hunting season and wandered to the bend in the river moving silently among the trees where the ravens were roosting. It was unlikely that with one shot I would bring down four and twenty drowsing blackbirds, but I might bring home enough for a smaller pie. My shot fired in the twilight struck nary a single bird.

Mom listened graciously to my report as she uncovered the steaming chicken pot pie she had just removed from the oven.

"Don't believe everything poets or cousins tell you," she said.

JUNE 17
Abbie

Most folks will agree that one should not have favorites among one's children or grandchildren. But I think it's acceptable on special days to favor one of the youngsters a bit more. Today Abbie is at the top of my list of favorite grandchildren. It's hard not to like Abbie even on those few days when she is only as good as the rest of us. But this day was made for her. Today was Abbie's day to stand tall—well, Abbie always stands tall. But I mean *tall* in the sense that today she has much to feel good about (with the exception of student loans and the price of education these days).

Abbie is among the Class of 2008. She has met the demands of four years of work, study, and peers, parents, and professors. And she did it her way. I like that. She emerged from it all with her integrity, self-esteem and million-dollar smile intact. Now with diploma in hand, licensed as an adult, she stands ready to seek her fortune in a crazy uncertain world. I am betting on Abbie.

If parents didn't have parents, children wouldn't have grandparents. Obvious, of course, but that is how Abbie came to be our granddaughter. It has been our good fortune and pleasure to watch Abbie grow from a gorgeous baby girl (I think God was at his creative best when He imagined little girls) to a rascally, spirited child to a beautiful young woman with a touch of Viking obstinacy and propensity to prefer her way. 　　　　　　　　　　　　　　　　＞＞＞

Abbie is smart, even wise. Smart enough to know how most things in this life work, but wise enough not to get entangled with the unsavory stuff out there. I might add, alert enough to have noticed that she is taller than I, but astute enough not to say so.

Abbie is going to make it. I am counting on it.

JUNE 18

Father's Day

The idea of Father's Day was proposed by a woman in Spokane, Washington. Although conceived originally in 1906, Fathers Day is a relatively recent phenomenon. Observed unofficially with varying enthusiasm since 1909, the idea was fully sanctioned by the U.S. president in 1972.

Consequently, my father was never the focus of Father's Day observances until his later years. He passed on in 1969. I never sent him a Father's Day card, but I do recall feeling remorseful at his funeral for not being more deliberate in my expressions of gratitude for his presence and care for me. In his later years, though not openly demonstrative, he treasured the family gatherings on his birthday, which in largely unspoken ways acknowledged his contributions to our lives.

My father is not here nor are my children (their cards and good wishes are in my luggage), but today is a special Father's Day. Pat and I are in London on our way to Norway, the birthplace of my father. His spirit travels with me.

I want to understand why he chose me to go with him to the fields with my own team of horses. Or brought me with him on construction projects and left my brothers to do the livestock chores. Or why he expected me to know better. "I thought you knew better than that," he would say.

In his unique Norwegian style he taught me how to do all kinds of things, which he probably learned to do there—how to use a square, hammer a nail straight, saw a board square, hold the other end of a cross-cut saw, cut and stack firewood, build barns, row a boat, and catch fish.

He said that it isn't necessary to talk all the time, reading books is not sissy stuff, one's worth isn't determined by how one makes a living, and your name is honorable—don't spoil it. Did the ambiance of the place instruct him?

He spoke longingly about the mountains, ocean, northern lights, and the midnight sun—phenomena quite foreign to children in mid-continent America.

I will see Norway with reminiscences of my father *flowing gentle on the rivers of my mind,* as the song goes.

JUNE 19

Old Promises

Sixty years ago today, I traveled by train on my way to a farm near a small town on the prairie in North Dakota. (Aren't all ND towns on the prairie?) Waiting there to greet me was the beautiful, bright, talented, young woman who had agreed that we should be married and merge our lives and dreams and embark on a journey that continues today. It was then and there that I met her family, extraordinarily gracious folks whose affirmation we cherish still.

The next day in the little Baptist church in the presence of Almighty God, families and friends, and we agreed without equivocation to commitments the magnitude of which we now more fully appreciate. The promises we made were ultimately only to each other, the gathered witnesses notwithstanding. That and a lot of magic and good luck have made all the difference.

We were young but it never occurred to us to question whether we were sufficiently mature to embark on an adventure the outcome of which was as uncertain as life itself. We both emerged from quite humble rural settings. Pat had completed one year of her first post-college professional assignment and I was a newly minted veteran of foreign wars. We were ready to seek our collective fortune, vague about the outcome but confident that, if it could be done, we could do it.

In the context of this counting of days advised by the Psalmist, 21,915 days have come and gone since that day decades ago.

JUNE 20

Days That Count

Obviously, as one's days on earth amass, the number of anniversaries one is obliged to acknowledge accumulates proportionately. There are countless firsts in one's life, that is, the time one took the first step or spoke the first word or received the first traffic ticket or kiss. These occasions may or may not be recorded, but they don't qualify as events that require annual remembrance. As exhilarating as a first kiss may seem, few normal folks rate its significance worthy of anniversary status.

Birth dates of spouses, parents, siblings, in-laws, children, grandchildren and great grandchildren along with those of favorite friends mark passages that we faithfully commemorate. As the years pass that inventory grows as the family expands. The accumulation of years also adds significance to what may have become perfunctory yearly rituals.

While the practice of commemorating milestones in life is totally optional, there is one major passage in life that I believe deserves, if not demands, spirited annual commemoration. Today was one of those days. Pat and I were sailing the North Sea on our way to Norway, a long overdue journey to the birthplace of my father. However momentous the voyage, it alone was not the source of our intense delight nor was the grandeur of the place. Fifty-eight years ago this day in a little North Dakota town next to nowhere we vowed (in the presence of God and other witnesses) to live our lives as one *with all the privileges, perquisites, and pitfalls pertaining thereto.*

When good things happen in our lives it is tempting to think we deserved them or that they were mostly of our own doing. Pat's personification of grace, patience, tolerance, quiet spirit, unconditional love, and a lot of luck notwithstanding, *Tis grace has brought us safe thus far.*

We dined in opulence overwhelmed by God's grace and his gift of fifty-eight, unforgettable years.

It was a good day!

JUNE 21

Still Counting

How do I love thee? Let me count the ways, the poet wrote.

I wonder how long the poet had been at it—telling of her love, that is. My love for you has outlasted my capacity to count new ways to tell of it. There can't be any end to the telling of it as long as we walk this earth together.

Can one tell of one's love without words? Roses tell it about as well as it can be told without words. But it seems that now, after these many years, roses have done their thing and words fail me. It is not that I have run out of words, it's the right words I search for. I could write a page of reasons why I love you.

Are there words that are more appropriate now than sixty years ago? I believe there are because then the notion of marriage was at best an ideal, an abstraction that one has to experience and live to understand. I know about love because you have taught me about love. You have loved me without condition. For sixty years you have been the personification of love. I have been embraced in an extraordinary demonstration of love, your love, a manifestation of love that cannot be sequestered with words. You have spoken your love unbounded by words. I love you for that!

What else can I say?

JUNE 22

Mozart, Merlot, and Midnight Sun

While hardly a connoisseur of good wine, I claim as inalienable the right to declare favorites. I have come to prize robust red wines, and not the least among them, merlots. It's unlikely that I could explain to the satisfaction of wine judges why merlot dominates my preferences, I just plain like it. But like all good things too commonly encountered, merlot at the wrong time or in the wrong place comes across no better than a common variety of red table wine. Context is critical.

My tastes in music range from Willie Nelson to Mozart. I will agree without serious debate that Mozart is a more suitable companion to merlot than Willie Nelson. Then there is this thing about context. I can't claim to have ever experimented or actively sought out an ideal context in which to enjoy the subtleties of a glass of merlot nor the harmonies of Mozart. It was serendipitous.

Pat and I were sailing (along with several hundred other travelers) above the Arctic Circle off the coast of Norway. We had come to experience Norway, the birthplace of my father, and to celebrate a major milestone in our lives together. Norway was every bit like the travelogues and brochures proclaimed it to be—cosmopolitan cities, spectacular scenery, charming cultural heritage, constantly changing land and seascapes, and near constant daylight.

As a child I listened with fascination and some skepticism to my father's animated accounts of the midnight sun. Scraps of my childhood skepticism seemed to have lodged in the deeper fissures of my mind. I wanted to see this thing of which my father spoke.

Late in the evening (after three days of clouds and fog as we sailed around the North Cape) I had retired to a lounge to enjoy a glass of merlot. Classical musicians doing their evening gig were playing Mozart. Mellow from the merlot, mindful of the Mozart, and musing about my father's depictions of the midnight sun, I was fearful the persistent fog would preclude a glimpse of the real thing.

Then serendipitously in the perfect context, as if nature was performing for me alone, the fog lifted, the clouds broke, and the midnight sun appeared brilliantly. I suppose it shone on others but I didn't notice. My eyes were misty.

My father was right!

JUNE 24

Gross Anatomy

For former students reminiscing with me about anatomy and zoology labs, the frog dissection exercise seems to be the mainstay of their memories. They chide me about my distinction between dissection and butchery. Their conversations recalled my very first attempt at dissection, which in retrospect, was more the latter than the former. And it was a toad, not a frog.

There was a large silo on the farmstead playground of my boyhood. In addition to the vast, above ground volume of the silo there was a portion, about four or five feet deep, below ground level. The space was declared off limits to my adventurous brothers and me for reasons which were vague until one day in the summer of 1932. My twin brother Harold, next brother Dick, and I ventured (actually jumped) into the below-ground depth of the silo, not concerned about our return to ground level. It was a great place to play tag with no corners in which to get trapped. It was a fascinating echo chamber where our yells and screams reverberated endlessly.

It wasn't until we realized, after tiring of running in circles and becoming hoarse from making echoes, that we were trapped in what had become a cold, damp dungeon. Our cries for rescue were silenced by the very echo chamber we had enjoyed. We waited for Mother subconsciously thinking that she, fully aware of her boys' potential to go where no boy had gone before, would know where to look. >>>

I busied my wait for rescue with a rather large toad I had noticed on the floor of our dungeon. When Mom came with a ladder, I put the toad in the pocket of my overalls, for what purpose I wasn't sure. While sitting on the edge of the porch to contemplate our misadventure, I remembered the toad.

Earlier that morning I had watched with more than casual interest my mother beheading, defeathering, and eviscerating chickens in preparation for our family dinner. Contemplating misadventure gets boring for a six-year old and I, mimicking my mother, set about doing the same to the toad with a rusting hacksaw blade conveniently left nearby. I had expertly severed the legs of the toad and about to begin the evisceration when Mom came to announce the time-out was over.

Obviously it was not over for me. I had additional time to wonder why (even though we didn't eat toads) big people could do things to chickens we couldn't do with toads. I didn't remind her that just last night Dad was reminiscing about a meal of frog legs he had once enjoyed.

I am glad she didn't know about our practice of removing the big legs of grasshoppers, our pretend cattle, to keep them from jumping over our toy fences.

JUNE 26

Pen Pal

A three-page, handwritten letter from 98-year-old Helga came in the mail today. Although I knew of her family I didn't know Helga. Her letter was precipitated by a book review of my recent book, The Improbable Professor. The piece in her local, small-town weekly caught her attention because it made reference to my grandfather, whose persona surfaces frequently throughout the book. She knew my long-deceased grandfather.

When Helga was younger—now nearly a century ago—her family lived as neighbors of my parents and grandparents. Her letter disclosed a lot of family history of which I was only vaguely aware. I learned that my Danish great grandmother (Bestemor) was also Helga's great aunt. She wrote that she had held me and tended to me when I was a babe. She told of her younger brothers (now gone) who moved in and out my life as a school child.

The interest of the early neighborly encounters notwithstanding, the truly remarkable aspect of this experience is Helga herself. "My name is Helga Matilda Lauritsen Wilson. Doesn't that have a ring to it?" she wrote. At 98, sound in body and mind, vibrant in spirit, one whose path crossed mine eight decades ago, she wanted me to know she remembered. I will write to Helga. I intend to nurture the relationship.

Everyone needs a *new* pen pal.

JUNE 28

As the Wheel Turns

News of the arrival of our newest great grandson came today. He is not our only great grandchild. Two cousins, who are now school children, preceded him. I am anxious to meet the little guy. Quite likely he will have a somewhat fetal look about him—all neonates do. However, careful scrutiny usually reveals, even at two days, hints of potential (good and bad) to look like someone in the clan.

This little one is the most recent edition to the fourth turn of our generational wheel. While the world becomes more complex and complicated, the wheel keeps turning and spinning off humans to inhabit an increasingly uninhabitable world. We oldsters ponder the future that will confront this child of our child's child. I am sure his parents (when not overwhelmed with diapers, feedings, and sleeplessness) do too. Not surprisingly, they without equivocation intend to keep him. Obviously, not to do so or even to have not imagined him is unimaginable.

I am glad he is here for all the reaches of human sentiment. But is it too naively optimistic that he and his generation may have solutions to the problems passing generations have created?

After all, he is our great grandson.

July

JULY 4

The Box

Last year about this time our extended family gathered at the round house to replace the weathered cedar shakes. Three generations all worked—some on the roof, others on the ground and in the kitchen. The task was finished on the evening of the Fourth of July and we celebrated with a sumptuous barbequed supper in the twilight. That this was very likely the last time we would do this task surfaced repeatedly in our conversation.

In the context of this numbering of days prompted by the Psalter, it's ironic that each major endeavor reminds us oldsters that this is or may be the last time we make this trip, purchase a new car, see a distant old friend, or paint the living room. Our days are, in fact, already numbered, which is not the main theme of the counting the ancient poet urges. His concern is the quality of the remaining days and that a bit of wisdom may accrue to the counter.

While some folks grown older are heard to say, "If I live long enough," most tend to avoid the observation that the number daily grows smaller. (Is grows smaller an oxymoron?) It has become apparent to me (and my fellow eighty-something folks, I suspect) that the fact of diminishing time begins to be a factor largely unspoken in decisions about multi-year magazine subscriptions, buying expensive shoes or remodeling the kitchen, for example. >>>

But I am certain it's not in the best interest of one's daily emotional tranquility to filter all of one's thoughts through a nagging awareness of time running out. Life is too short for that.

This is a time to think beyond the box.

JULY 5

The Day after Yesterday

Today is, as is every day, the day after yesterday. It's the 5th of July—the day after the Fourth of July. This day doesn't carry with it the same set of images as does the Fourth of July, another illustration of the unlucky standing in the shadow of greatness. The 5th of July really doesn't have much to shout about. One wonders what those guys, who chose to make July 4th what it is, did on the 5th of July. Probably, they wrote letters.

I have never, so far as I can remember, written a letter or anything else on the 5th of July, which now that I think of it may have contributed no little bit to the insignificance of the day. There are all too many seemingly insignificant days in life, so I hereby declare the 5th of July a significant day. Whatever significance accrues to the day because I wrote this will be for whomever reads this to decide.

The ancient poet wrote: *This is the day that the Lord hath made. Rejoice and be glad in it. It* in this case means, I suppose, the day the writer has in mind. The only thing about that day of which we can be certain is that it was a day following some other day. In our attempts to make these scriptural bits of truth and wisdom relevant to our lives, we have concluded that this particular declaration (given that God is the giver of days) applies to all of our days. That is, I believe, what is significant about this day—the 5th of July.

That causes me to rejoice.

JULY 6

Downsizing Dogma

Leaving behind the accumulated stuff of life is unavoidable in the exit lane. One simply does not need much of the stuff once thought to be unequivocally essential and perhaps at some time was. It is relatively easy to abandon material things that have, because of physical limitations, long fallen into disuse, for example my in-line skates.

An unexpected aspect to this downsizing, however, is the discovery of a lot of intellectual baggage once thought crucially important to one's intellectual integrity and prestige. One recognizes that notions once so essential to the defense of intellectual high ground turn out to have been quite arbitrary all along, especially those pertinent to the ideological turfdoms that professors so zealously defend. Although we treat ideological constructions as real entities, they are at best quite ephemeral and more transient than many of us are willing to admit. Our security in this economy of ideas depended on the durability of our ideological superstructures.

That was then. Life in the realm of ideas was exciting, challenging and rewarding. But the contours of that domain have changed and I am only an interested but otherwise uninvolved, bystander. While it may afford me a bit of intellectual tranquility I no longer have use for my assemblage of facts and ideas about molecules, genes, and cells. But it's the dogma that won't stay behind.

I can't find the delete key.

JULY 8

Rigs & Rigness

Stopped by what seemed an unusually long red light, I noticed that four of every five vehicles in line were pickup trucks giving credence to the claim that our region is peak pickup domain, where pickups are invariably and affectionately referred to as one's rig. A while back a local columnist wrote confessing his disquiet because his vehicle didn't inspire him to think of it as a rig. That rigness is not a quality intrinsic in vehicles seems not to have occurred to him. But I have known for a long time that it's the driver who puts that mark on one's vehicle.

My grandfather called his buggy and his team of sorrel ponies named Maude and Molly his rig. Given the contemporary penchant to equate rig with machismo one might argue that Jack and Jim would have been a more appropriate team for a genuine rig. Nonetheless, when my grandfather—a sturdy, stately, Danish immigrant—stepped into his carriage it was without debate a rig. As I recall, sitting in my grand-father's seat pretending to be him simply did not conjure the same image. My ability to impart rigness to my conveyances came later.

There are vehicles that defy rig status. My father's 1928 Essex was like that. That Essex refused to run only long enough to get us away from home and then abandon us. My father was not the sort of guy who expected his car to inflate his self-esteem. He was a ruggedly handsome fellow who added considerable character to every car he drove, but somehow that Essex seemed to defy him. He called it a lot of things but never did he call it his rig. Except for that Essex, all of my dad's vehicles were rigs, especially his 1926 Buick Master. I remember hearing the townsfolk say when he drove by, "There's Ole's rig." I don't recall anyone saying that about anyone else's Buick.

I have driven vehicles of various vintages and sizes, all of which became rigs when I drove. Even our postwar 1948 Wylis Jeep pickup acquired definite rig status when I drove it, although when standing idle it seemed to be struggling desperately to look like one.

The only debate about whether any of my vehicles was a rig came from a careless college student who, like many contemporary young guys, was convinced that rig status requires four-wheel drive and grotesquely over-sized tires. "An S-10 is not a rig," he foolishly proclaimed, questioning the status of my small Chevy truck. Even Pat, who pays little attention to the emotional baggage with which men encumber their vehicles, acknowledges the rigness of that little beauty.

It's not what your rig can do for you. It's what you can do for your rig.

JULY 10

Back on the Ground

The local news sheet announced the tour stop in town of a World War II B-17 bomber. As the Flying Fortress was the airframe in which I did my part of that Great War, I decided to relive a bit of history and to inspect the grand old aircraft in which I had spent significant hours of my later teenage years. Airframe is contemporary jargon meaning airplanes flown by today's military pilots of which Grandson Jordan is one. He taught me to say airframe when I mean airplane.

I invited the younger, down-the-street grandkids to come with me to impress them with my familiarity of this old war machine. Subconsciously perhaps, I wanted them to sense the images that linger in my aging mind. The visions of glory and glamour that ricocheted in my mind at the sight of this memorable airplane didn't emerge for the kids. They seemed at best mildly impressed. The intensity of my experiences in the inner spaces of the plane seemed not to transfer to them as they moved with ease through the constricted passages of the interior, which seem to have been and probably were designed for 150 pound 18-year-olds.

As I viewed my daughter's photo record of the occasion, I realized what was wrong with the picture. The stately old plane was unchanged, but there is no place in the scenario for 80-year-old, one-time, tail gunners gotten too girthy to move comfortably through the limited walkways. Looking back is not the same for veterans as it is for their grandkids.

Perhaps it's best for old airmen to stay on the ground.

JULY 15
Like Him

Today, sensing this could well be our last visit to Minneapolis (this great city that was home during significant years in younger days) we toured the areas in which we had lived, worked, studied, and moved about freely decades ago. Especially imposing are the changes in the metropolitan center where the college I was attending had been located. Grand new hotels, municipal buildings, corporate head quarters, theaters, educational institutions, and sport stadia adorn the area. Gone are the streetcars, the rescue missions and the transients (bums or derelicts as they were called then) along with my alma mater where I had enrolled in ministerial studies a couple of months prior to my 27th birthday. I was going to be a preacher. That didn't happen, but that's another story.

The college was religiously conservative and pragmatic in its requirements. All students were assigned experiences intended to prepare them for their chosen work. Nearly ten years older than my classmates with a look of maturity (my coal-black hair revealed a bit of encroaching gray) I was given the more adult assignments. I was sent to preach to the bums at the downtown Gospel Mission. About seventy-five men in various stages of weariness, hunger, wellness, cleanness, attentiveness, and soberness sat waiting impatiently for their supper, while I honed my homiletic skills. As was the custom, at the end of my talk I invited any who might wish to talk more about what I had said to meet me up front—secretly hoping, I confess, that no one would.

But one fellow, seemingly uncertain about why, came to talk to me. Distracted, I believe, by my appearance at the pulpit (tanned and conditioned by construction work on non-class days, comfortable in suit and tie, articulate and scholarly in demeanor, and handsome—more imagined than actual) his wish was, "I want to be like you."

I don't remember my words to him, but I remember my thoughts. You don't want to be like me. You, and I as well, should want to be like Him, whose Gospel I was sent here to proclaim.

I never went back there to preach again. I wasn't ready.

JULY 16

Thoughts About Thinking

In the verbal intercourse of professors one frequently hears references to thinking people. Given the tendency of professors to be a bit elitist we, without thinking, count ourselves among that class of persons. Perhaps all self-respecting persons do too. I confess that I did. The designation of some persons as thinking people implies that there are non-thinking people. In the academic arena they are probably the ones who do not agree with the professor making the distinction.

Thinking is as essential as breathing. If there are differences among persons regarding thinking, it is probably not whether they think or don't think, but what they think about. Certainly there are persons who are busy thinking about something other than what professors are thinking about, but to call them non-thinking seems to me arbitrarily dismissive. Ordinary people (those whom professors likely don't include in their category of thinking people) probably won't have the professorial luxury of thinking about things that don't matter. For instance, thinking about thinking.

Having been a professor, that is, a thinking person, now retired and no longer having any need to judge folks on the merits of their mental agility, I have indulged in some thinking about thinking. This is what I think. Thinking is a lot of things: decision making, problem solving, creativity—writing blurbs such as this. >>>

However, the real essence of thinking is, I think, the content of the constant conversations one has with oneself about oneself (stuff other than abstractions, such as weather, politics, religion, etcetera). I have concluded that one's emotional tranquility rests entirely on the quality of these private conversations. One of the perquisites of retirement is that it affords one an uncluttered mind conducive to quality confabulation with oneself—the sort of quiet idle musing that causes curious companions to want to buy into the conversation. "A penny for your thoughts," they say.

Given current inflation, admission to these thoughts ought to be at least a dollar, I think.

JULY 19

Ramschackle Dreams

Our house is situated at the foot of a steep, rocky strip of fir and pine forest. While actually in the suburbs, it is remote and quiet. Our street is delightfully devoid of traffic. We have grown accustomed to watching an array of wildlife move through the scene from our living room windows. The feature of this season is the romping of white tail fawns, one of which we spotted yesterday hidden by its mother ten feet from our deck.

A favorite expedition into these woods was with grandchildren to explore an abandoned, primitive house unlived in for decades. Like with many families, our grandkids arrived in waves. And each new set, in turn, was introduced to the Three Bears' House, as it became known because of the discovery of three chairs, one of which was broken.

The grandchildren have all outgrown the myth, and visits to the place are now legend. Sadly, our local, in-town, one-year-old, great grandson Karsten, who was next-in-line to visit the Three Bears' House will not join the legend. His mother was the first to explore the site with us and probably spotted the broken chair and imagined the story. My fantasy was to take him there.

Unfortunately, the encroachment of ubiquitous development is changing it all. We had assumed the steep rocky terrain was too ill suited for building. Not so. The old house is gone.

In its place stands a $500,000 modern chalet, the product of money, engineering, and progress, thwarting Karsten's and my journey into the story.

Thus ended the dream.

JULY 20

Sarpy Creek

With the majority of our immediate families in the midwest we have motored to Minnesota from Spokane and back again more times then we care to admit. Without going all the way around the back side of the earth one cannot travel by land from here to there directly (or back again) without traversing Montana. There are a lot of interstate miles in Montana and we have been over them all so many times that even the smaller bumps are readily recognized. Aptly named Big Sky country, Montana has a lot of everything: mountains, rivers, prairies, cattle, creeks, big sky, and endless interstate miles.

Montana's DOT, in an effort to inform motorists of their progress traversing the vast areas of nothing but sky and grass in eastern Montana, has placed signs naming the innumerable creeks over which one drives. I know them all and can tell fellow travelers which will be the next one we will encounter. Some of the more memorable are Sad Woman Creek, Dead Horse Creek, Bad Road Creek, Dry Creek (an oxymoron), Whoopup Creek, and Sarpy Creek.

While driving through Big Sky country may seem to be mindless activity, it is not. One has countless moments to contemplate the origin of these colorful creek monikers. And I have done that. I suspect that some legendary streambank person or event inspired these names. I could, of course, inquire of the local historical societies about the source of these descriptive tags, but that would unduly extend my time in Montana.

I have my own ideas about the inspiration of the legends, which I refine on each additional drive over these streambeds. I think I know why the lady was sad and what killed the horse and why Bad Road was bad. But Sarpy? I have no idea.

And today's passage didn't help.

JULY 23

Geezers, etcetera

A friend, a fellow a few years older than I, bought a CB radio to amuse himself while driving on the nation's interstate highways. He kept his receiver tuned to frequencies used by long distance truck drivers and eavesdropped on their chatter. He recounted a conversation between two drivers attempting to travel together. The conversation went something like this: "Hey Crankshaft, Where are you? My mirrors don't show you."

"It's OK, Turbo. I'll catch up soon as I get around this geezer and his Buick."

Just then Rich noticed a big rig changing lanes to pass. It's not uncommon to see an elderly citizen driving a Buick. It's the car of choice among geezers.

But this is about neither Buicks nor geezers per se. It's about my more than mild disquiet about the pejorative vocabulary commonly used to caricaturize nice old guys like me —words like geezer, codger, fogy, fuddy-duddy, curmudgeon; words that may be, but don't necessarily have to be, prefaced by old. A search for synonyms turns up adjectives like churlish, irascible, cantankerous, crabby, disreputable, irritable, eccentric. Guys of any age can and do display attitudes or behavior implied by those words. It's unlikely that I have never been a bit churlish, but I can't accept the notion that old guys are so much more disposed to unpleasantry that special words with the innuendo are required. Furthermore, with the exception of biddy, there are no comparable words used in references to old women.

I try to avoid the drift towards geezerliness. I am fortunate. Pat subtly alerts me to evidence of any such tendency. Recently she noticed me perusing a brochure featuring new model Buicks. "Don't die and leave me with a Buick," she said

She prefers to ride into the sunset in our old Honda.

JULY 24

Nostology

In the land of letters among academicians where I spent most of my adult years, it was my fate to attend innumerable faculty and committee meetings. A decade of retirement has purged from me most of the cynicism engendered by the scramble for recognition and position in the meritocratic posturing that marred many of these capers. However, honesty restrains me from declaring my innocence in the participation in that nonsense. I could pontificate with the best.

There was, as I recall, a lot of comedy in that arena, much of it unintended. One antic that never failed to amuse me was the apparent need to establish one's credibility. It was fashionable, or perhaps thought expedient, to preface one's profundities with a reference to one's credentials.

One of my least favorite colleagues invariably prefaced his comments with "sociologically speaking." (I know, having least favorite colleagues is a luxury not afforded by our Creator—I am working on that.) Others, just as predictably, would speak "theologically, politically, or philosophically." I can say with assurance I was never tempted to speak "biologically."

It's remarkable how quickly the significance of the intellectual trappings of academic turfdoms fade once one enters the exit lane purged of one's repository of abstractions.

But perhaps I am only speaking "nostologically."

JULY 25

Remembering Me

In these late inning days the routines of oldsters like me seem to be interrupted ever more frequently by the call to gather with others of our cohort (unceremoniously dubbed the dying generation by my friend, Dave) to acknowledge the passing and to commemorate the life of another of our friends. Not unlike many of our cultural rites, these ceremonies have fallen into a predictable pattern of sameness. This is not intended as a critique, just an observation refined by frequent exposure.

One can imagine that persons dealing with grief or relief from contending with the arduous care of suffering loved ones may not be at their creative best. I have on occasion left a farewell ceremony troubled by the thought that the departed deserved better. You may well wonder whether I am concerned that those to whom it falls to memorialize me can do it well and stay within the bounds of truth. Not to worry, I say. I have lived intimately with three of the most creative and imaginative persons on earth—my wife and daughters.

Given my proclivity for introspection and my incorrigible vanity, I am too often distracted during celebrations of persons departed and project myself into that inevitable scenario, wondering how they—the folks to whom it matters most—will want others to remember me. I resist the urge to advise them.

Perhaps my concern should be less about the send-off here and more about the greeting there.

JULY 26

Neologisms Notwithstanding

If one has a predisposition toward eccentricity it will probably become more obvious as time passes, which may be (now that I think about it) tantamount to suggesting that all elders are more or less eccentric. I won't deny my peculiarities. I enjoy reading the dictionary. In fact, I am not at all reticent about my addiction to neology. Why use familiar words when there are so many interesting alternatives?

However, some strange ironies do emerge when one wanders out of the abstract realm of words into the real world of life and death. In these extra-inning years we contend more intimately with the immediacy of being and not being.

Each day, it seems, we learn of some fellow sojourner being challenged by the dreaded invasion of malignant cells. The dictionary defines neoplasm, the word we employ to denote the unwanted mass, as a new growth of tissue having no useful physiological function (from the Greek word neos— new plus plasma—something formed; literally new formation). Neology at it's best.

While I was reading N words last evening, I was interrupted with the news that a friend was near the end of this ironic struggle between new cells with no useful physiological function and old cells with an intense desire to live.

Whether one talks in euphemisms or neologisms, it still hurts.

JULY 27

I Gotta Be Me

There seems to be etched in the human psyche a sense that each of us is unique, distinctly different from every other human being. As a student of genetics I can submit evidence that each of the several billions of us (excepting identical twins) is indeed sole holder of a unique combination of genes (DNA molecules) unlikely to be duplicated by natural processes. Genes notwithstanding, each of us will insist that no one can ever know what it is like to be me. One's thoughts, feelings, hopes, hurts, and joys—the stuff of one's inner self is unequivocally one's alone. We are, one might say, all unrepeatable variations of a universal theme.

The collective human endeavor, it seems to me, is to manage all this incredible, incomprehensible variety without compromising the uniqueness and integrity of each of us. History reveals that we have not done that well.

You may wonder why I, a sojourner well along on the journey, ramble on about what is obvious to most observant people. I have been fortunate. I have lived in this land of freedom, bounty and opportunity and arrive a far piece down the road with my physical, emotional, mental, and spiritual self quite intact. And I will admit for the most part I have been allowed, as the song goes, to do it my way.

But I confess that I am a bit fearful that, good genes and good fortune notwithstanding, the time may come when my "I gotta be me" attitude may have to be checked.

I surely hope not. Until the end, I wanna be me!

JULY 29

A Holy Hello

It was a bright summer sky filled with billowing, cumulus clouds. A friend and his grandson Andrew were casually cruising along country roads when the boy, who had been resting his head on the windowsill gazing at the clouds, murmured, "Hi, God!" The boy was not the first nor will he be the last to be in awe of the vastness and grandeur of the sky and sense the presence of God.

While it may not conjure an awareness of the Creator, the enormity of all that space and stuff out there must mystify even the most indifferent observers. I do wonder to what extent the idea of God-Creator lingers in the thoughts of oldsters who must, occasionally at least, ponder what comes next. Few of them talk much about it except perhaps on the threshold of their departure. Some sense of uneasiness about the meaning of it all, however, must enter the thought streams of even the most stoic.

While denying being obsessed about finality, I will admit to entertaining thoughts about the outcome of my tenure in this context more frequently than I was wont to do when I was busy with the essentials of life in the here and now. I can't remember a time when God was not part of my mental rumination. From boyhood prayers at Mother's side on through the intensity of my professional life in the realm of ideas, notions about the nature of God have been integral in my sense of reality. I have considered all the images that religion and theological professionals have invented to describe the indescribable and have set them aside as humanly limited efforts to understand the incomprehensible. Without a lot of anxiety about the precision of my perceptions of God, I have grown comfortable with a profound sense of His presence.

That frequently prompts me to murmur with Andrew, "Hi God!"

August

AUGUST 1
Flies

While contemplating a letter to grandson Jordan, I noticed a housefly on my study window. Flies do strange things. This one inspired this note to Jordan, who flies with the Air Force.

> Hey Jordan,
>
> Did I ever teach you a song I learned somewhere back in antiquity? I may have learned it while in the army. The song is about flies (flies the noun, not flies the verb). I was reminded of it when I saw your flyguy@wherever e-mail moniker. The main refrain goes like this: "There may be flies on some of you guys, but there ain't no flies on me." Now that I think about it, the song has only one refrain, which incidentally is true of most popular songs.
>
> If the song has any merit, I suppose it is that life is good when you can't think of anything that is your fault. I am having one of those days, that is, when I can't think of anything that is my fault. However, I can easily think of a lot of things that other guys think are my fault, but they are probably trying to put their flies on me.
>
> Life is besieged with flies both actual and figurative. We have mechanisms to screen them out, but sometimes the door gets left open and we become one of the guys with flies on him. I know. I have had flies.
>
> Fighting flies is a lifelong task. I am always troubled by TV images of the faces of starving refugee children

crawling with flies, who are unable to shoo them away. It is, indeed, tragic when one gets to the place where it doesn't matter, or one doesn't care, or doesn't have the strength or energy to brush the flies away. More so when one doesn't notice one's own flies. Perhaps that's the message of the song and I ought to quit singing it.

Watch out for the flies, FlyGuy.

AUGUST 3

Duh

From the time I was a boy I wanted to be a farmer like my father and grandfather. In the first few years of our life together Pat and I pursued my dream on her family's wheat farm. Late one summer the local school board members, farmers themselves suspecting that as a wheat farmer I had little to do during the non-growing season, urged me to consider teaching the children in the little school house a mile from the edge of our farm. There was one catch. I lacked the proper credentials.

Not a problem, they said. The State Department of Education would issue an emergency teaching certificate to anyone who passed an examination currently held at the county seat. Encouraged by Pat, I wrote and passed the exam. Ten days later I was schoolmaster of eight children scattered over five grades. I still remember their names. Violet, Vernon, Frieda, Rachael, John, Agnes, Oscar, and Louise.

The younger children labored with reading, writing, spelling, and numbers—major effort for kids who spoke only German in their homes. The older pupils grappled with the basic propositions of language, history, geography, arithmetic, and natural science, an endeavor hampered no little bit because for them English was also a second language. In retrospect it was a delightful experience, frequently enlivened by Johnny's attempts to translate his thoughts into English. Wondering about the outcome of a spelling contest he asked, "What if we all both every day miss one?"   >>>

There in those dark winter days in that North Dakota school house (there was no electricity to light the room) I began to ponder my preoccupation with farming. I became curious about the intellectual scenarios Pat described when reminiscing about her college days. So after several years we left the farm resolved to return someday, and at the age of twenty-six I enrolled in college.

A few years later, deep into doctoral studies, I encountered a foreign language requirement. I had to learn to read German. Pat had attended that very same small school when she was a child. She had learned German from her grandmother. With her patient and skillful tutoring I passed the test. Only then did it occur to me that perhaps I should have let my young pupils teach me German. That may have been the easier way.

Like our German farmer neighbor would say, "Ve get too soon oldt undt too late schmart."

AUGUST 5

My Words

The dictionary is one of my favorite books. Pat says that I am the only one she knows who reads the dictionary in bed before going to sleep. While that is not entirely true, I have been known to read my dictionary just for pleasure. Therefore, I read with interest (and pleasure) a piece in a journal whose function it is to review professional and literary writing much of which is largely wordsmithing, which not infrequently obscures the message especially for vocabulary challenged persons. See Ecclesiastes 6:7. *The more the words the less the meaning thereof.*

What I read today was a delightfully written, informative piece about the first and subsequent editions of the Oxford English Dictionary, originally conceived in 1857. Not only did I come away with new appreciation for the book but a newfound justification for my intrigue with it.

Words have always fascinated me. As my professorial escapades matured I became growingly aware of words and how the choice and ordering of words lend nuances of humor, satire, interest, and excitement to sentences even in the context of rather mundane subjects like the practices and protocols of professors. It was really that challenge and my delight with words that lured me to the computer and fueled my fantasies about being a writer.

Everyone comes to own a vocabulary which literally becomes a window into one's mind and soul. One might argue that scrolling though one's personal collection of words offers glimpses of one's physical, intellectual, emotional and spiritual history—perhaps even more so than scrutiny of one's DNA sequences. My repository of words includes a collage of words both literary and technical. The latter are now largely unemployed except in our frequent Scrabble games. *Zygotic* is a big winner.

Dizygotic, a variation also found in my personal cache, conjures images of real intimacy. After all, my closest brother was (before everything else) my wombmate.

AUGUST 8
Trucks

One week after I returned home from soldiering in WWII I began a job driving a truck. It was an old, long-wheelbase, flatbed International with a powerful and noisy engine used to move ground corn or alfalfa to railroad cars, distilleries, or animal feed suppliers. While not giving much thought about future careers or vocation, for the next several months I was a truck driver loading and unloading 100 lb. sacks of milled corn and alfalfa. It was hard work. It involved the heavy lifting my grandfather promised me I could avoid if I became a professor. There were no forklifts then, but I rather liked the work and driving the big, old, noisy truck. I imagined owning my own truck and beginning a trucking company.

When another hometown veteran and I learned that my truck was for sale our imaginations soared. Trucks were scarce in the post-war economy and we would buy the truck, operate it night and day, earn a lot of money, buy another one and that would be the start of our trucking business. Believing that the local bankers were sympathetic to aspiring veterans we naively invited them to finance our dream; after all we had successfully defended their free enterprise economy. They essentially laughed us out the door, thus ending that dream.

I am still fascinated by trucks. I have a warm spot in my heart for truckers. Bankers conjure other emotions. Often as I sit at my computer by our study window which faces the street, my reverie is interrupted by trucks of many sizes and function as they move to several construction sites up and down our streets. I admire the skill with which these guys maneuver their rigs and manipulate the labor saving attachments. And I say, "Hey, I could do that!"

I have driven perhaps as many trucks as any other non-professional driver. In my farmer-rancher life I drove grain and cattle trucks. On several different occasions I have driven U-Drive trucks half-way across our nation. Driving a ten-axle rig across the nation is not necessarily mindless activity, but it does afford one countless hours of contemplation. While I no longer have any attraction to that role, I have special admiration for over-the-road truck drivers who do and, not unlike pensioners, spend a lot of time looking back.

I wonder what stories their rearview mirrors tell.

AUGUST 10

First Wine

A friend, a connoisseur, brought me a bottle of fine wine today. Mellowed from savoring his gift my mind drifted to my introduction to the fruit of the vine.

It was a lovely spring day in Italy. Bill, my best army buddy, had the day off from bombing missions as did I. We were hiking in the countryside near the air base and stopped by a country railroad station for some rest in the shade of olive trees and a drink of cool water from a well from which neighboring families drew water.

While we lingered there two children arrived at the well carrying a bucket I thought was too large for them. They carefully drew water from the well with a rope and smaller pail. When their container was full the girl fashioned a towel to cushion her head and stooped down as the little boy attempted to lift the bucket to her head. They spilled most of the water and once again filled their pail. Attempting to raise the pail to her head a second time they spilled the water. The boy was too short to raise the pail to her head and he was too small to carry it on his. We marveled at their tenacity. They filled the pail again, reluctant it seemed to bring home less than a full pail of water.

Before they could spill it again I volunteered to carry the water for them. They chattered excitedly and ran skipping ahead of me towards a complex of buildings about 400 yards away. As we neared the houses, what seemed to be three generations of folks hurried to meet us exclaiming, "Gracias! Gracias Joe!" (All GIs were Joe.) Then the patriarch handed me a bottle of white wine.

Back at the station Bill, a devotee of a strict religious tradition, asked me what I was going to do with it. God would be displeased if I drank it, he insisted. Risking God's disapproval, Bill's displeasure, and innocent about the effects of wine I drank all of it there in the shade of the olive trees. (It was a small bottle.) My only previous taste of wine was a few snitched sips of Dad's home-vinted chokecherry wine.

Bill has forgiven me. I still enjoy the warmth of his friendship as well as that from a glass of merlot. And I believe God is OK with that.

But nothing warms one's soul like helping a kid in trouble. Of that both God and Bill approve.

AUGUST 12

Red Wagon

Dear Suzanne,

A little arithmetic discloses that you are about to complete the first year of the second fifty years of your earthly sojourn. That I had to do the arithmetic suggests a couple of disturbing thoughts. Has the accumulation of years become so unbelievably large that it requires verification? Or is the significance of the event in some way proportional to the number? If the latter is true, one should be certain the number is correct to insure the birthday wishes are not inappropriate. Should what one wished for a yearling on her first birthday differ from what one would hope for her on the first birthday of the second half?

I remember two things about that first birthday celebration. We gave you the little red wagon. Ever wonder why we wanted you, a little girl, to have a red wagon? That I had wanted a wagon when I was a child may have influenced our decision. About the only things you could do with the wagon was to sit in it and walk around it, which you learned to do that day. I wonder if we expected you to haul things in it. After all, that's what wagons are for and that's what I would have done with the wagon I never had. I remember envisioning you riding in the wagon and me pulling it ready to take you wherever you wished to go. But you learned to walk that day and at least on that day preferred to walk around the wagon rather than ride in it—an early indication of your will to "do it my lone."

›››

I used to argue that symbols were in the category of ideas that have no independent or objective existence. Symbols become real when they become associated with some object like a wagon. In retrospect, I believe the significance of your wagon was more symbolic than practical. I am not implying that, however impractical, the wagon was not a good gift for a one-year-old. It was a good gift even though we may not have realized its real significance at the time.

Wagons are for carrying burdens. What burdens do one-year-olds have for which they need a wagon? Burdens come later as does the realization that we all need some assistance with our loads. Being totally convinced that much of what we do is intuitive, usually not consciously aware of the mental forces that shape our decisions, I would like to believe that with the wagon your mother and I were saying the road that lies ahead of you, our lovely and lively one-year-old, is long and you will encounter encumbrances with which you will need assistance. Start with this red wagon. We will help you pull it, if need be.

Now some number of years later, I wonder what is appropriate to say to you having pulled your wagon, sometimes heavily laden, a far piece along that road. I think I will offer you a new red wagon (symbolic, of course) with sturdy brakes with which to carry the more weighty encumbrances of life on the downhill part of the road. My wish for you is that this wagon will be laden with happiness, fulfillment, and above all peace.

And love—our love. Happy Birthday!

AUGUST 13

Ancient Ways

There is a lot of sameness about South Dakota. The scattered farmsteads mostly treeless afford a bit of variety, but the rolling prairie landscape, beautiful in its own subtle way, seems endless. Having been to Mt. Rushmore, the Black Hills, the Bad Lands, Wall Drug, the Corn Palace, and rallied with the bikers at Sturgis, most of our travels in South Dakota now days are on our way to someplace else.

Today, as we were making our way across South Dakota on our way home from someplace else, we approached a group of people by their cars stopped on the edge of the highway. It was a typical SD panorama—endless, seemingly vacant prairie, no trees, no fences, and no towns, just sky and grass. Obviously something unusual had caused these folks to stop.

Curious, we slowed and learned as we made our way through the scenario that a very young whitetail fawn had been struck and left for dead by a speeding motorist indifferent to life God created to be in this place. The small creature, although badly hurt, was still alive and was fortunately rescued by caring folks from further abuse by oblivious motorists on their way to someplace else. Whether it survived we don't know. What we do know is that these creatures of God were there long before we invaded their space with too little regard for the ancient paths they instinctively follow.

The prophet Jeremiah advises his readers to *Stop at the crossroads and look for the ancient paths, where the good way lies.* >>>

It may be obvious, as some may argue, that Jeremiah wasn't advising modern travelers to look around as they hurry on to someplace else.

But then perhaps he was.

AUGUST 14
Genes, Generations, & Genealogy

The Bible passages recording the lineages of significant people, which we read in Sunday School and later in college classes, are lightheartedly referred to as "the begats." The word *begat* is archaic and probably most familiar to adherents of the King James translation of the Bible. But I like the word. It's rather devoid of emotion, carries with it no sense of responsibility. It simply records that Soanso was the father of Soanso II, and that he, in turn, was the father of Soanso III.

The word *begat* has fallen out of favor, but the activity so denoted shows no signs of demise. According to present day demographers, begatting is as popular as ever. It is proceeding unabashedly and without abatement. Nowhere is that more apparent than at family reunions.

Today, the 123rd anniversary of my father's birth, persons from five generations of his descendants gathered for a family reunion. A lot of people (70-100, no one attempted an accurate count) from one-month-old babes to octogenarians appeared. One clear conclusion about the group became evident that no little begatting has been going on.

Pat and I drove 1,500 miles to be there. Others also traveled far to be there. Except for an unspoken sense of belonging to a fading heritage, I pondered the motivation of the younger ones for whom recollections of the patriarch are faint or legendary and whose allegiance to the heritage varies extensively. A student of genetics, I searched for visible evidence of the common gene pool, or as I am disposed to say in moments of immodesty "our mutual gene pool." (There is nothing common about our genes.) One could see similarities within families but likeness between families was less obvious. If these 70-plus family folks were scattered among several hundred other people, it's not likely many of them would be instantly recognized as descendents of the grand patriarch. Generations of begatting does indeed produce interesting and delightful variants, but in the process there is the inevitable natural dilution of the gene pool.

Nevertheless, if one would be attentive to attitude, I think one would detect some commonalities. There seems to be a pervasive "Show me!" stance or an "I can do it!" posture—but also (unfortunately, I think) an indifference or suspicion about some of the finer aspects of language, mind, and spirit. The latter are dimensions of life that are important to me, but which seem to have bypassed some of the begotten.

Begatting happens!

AUGUST 15

Extra Innings

There are a number of metaphors with which one might speak or write about that period of life commonly referred to as old or advanced age. I have used them all and indulge myself with the fantasy that I may have invented some of them. These familiar everyday analogies are useful when attempting to speak or write sensitively about old people or people on the way there.

Folks who move merrily about life a bit more slowly perhaps, unconcerned that they have reached the actuarial life expectancy of people in their demographic cluster, may be likened to pokey drivers in the fast lane oblivious of the imminent exit lane.

Bonus, the word, implies something unexpected or in addition to, sometimes with the inference that what was received was not necessarily merited. People who defy health challenges and emerge from end-of-life crises may be said to be living in bonus years and may be the ones of whom the Psalmist thought when he wrote: *The days of our years are threescore and ten; and if by strength they be fourscore*. It is those days after the threescore and ten, which seem to be conditional. I no longer use bonus years to denote post threescore-and-ten people lest I suggest these folks may have gotten away with something.

Sports analogies are helpful in these conversations—late in the fourth quarter, overtime, or sudden death all conjure up notions of finality. As does extra innings, which I like in that it suggests second chances. But my favorite is the double innuendo of a scene depicting an octogenarian painter on the top rung of an extension ladder stretching off balance to reach the edge while whistling Nearer my God to Thee.

I don't think I am obsessed with apocalyptic scenarios; it is just that that they are everywhere. Today the World Series game lasted 15 innings.

I wonder. When does life go to extra innings or overtime?

AUGUST 19

Imperfection

During worship services today the ministers conducted a brief ceremony in which the parents and the congregation dedicated themselves to give careful attention to the spiritual welfare of a little boy. The ceremony progressed smoothly and to the extent that these events can be judged I believe it was considered successful. The keeping of the covenant is a story yet to be written and the ritual will be forgotten by most of us bystanders. The little boy, too young to remember, will only learn of it in review.

Like most regular churchgoers I have witnessed scores of baptismal ceremonies, but also like most regulars can describe few of them in any detail. I observed one such event three decades ago that invariably flutters through my mind as I watch and listen to this rite. On this special Sunday some caring people brought several seriously mentally defective persons to church and probably unwisely seated them in the very front pew. The service was long and these unfortunate individuals, totally unaware of where they were, grew restless and noisy with sounds more animal than human. One could sense the unease move through the congregation.

Into this setting parents brought their perfectly developed infant to be baptized. While the minister conducted the ceremony flawlessly despite the distraction, the dissonance was palpable made more intense in my mind because we had earlier in the service heard the words of the Psalmist who declared: *For you created my inmost being; you knit me together in my mother's womb. I praise you because I am fearfully and wonderfully made; your works are wonderful, I know that full well.*

OK, Lord, but what about the worshippers in the front row?

AUGUST 20

The Paradox of Progress

As I waited my turn at the dentist's office today, I watched the assistant measure the height of a child. She asked him to stand against a wall on which was painted a tape marked in inches. The child was 54 inches tall for which the nurse complimented him. The boy seemed pleased but couldn't disguise his apprehension about the impending dental exam.

Still waiting my turn (not at the measuring tape, since progress in that parameter for old timers is not of interest to dentists) my thoughts turned to the fixation we humans seem to have with progress. We measure everything. Schools record the learning progress of our kids by grades 1-12. Then later academic degrees, certification, licensing, etcetera. We measure success in terms of sales, income, books, rank, and votes. Life becomes a contest with standards.

We oldsters (done with progress in education, professional striving, social status, and personal betterment) still function in a milieu of standards. But our competition is not the universe out there. It's the world within. We contend with standards indicating levels, ranges, and limits of our physical, mental, and emotional well being. One might say we are measured post-progress or by whatever the antonym of progress is—regress I suppose.

The tension between progress and aging notwithstanding, the standards by which I measure (count) my extra inning days are peace, tranquility, contentment, expectation, confidence, triumph, assurance and amusement.

These are standards I can live with.

AUGUST 25

Broken Circle

In my short career as a minister I was called on to perform wedding ceremonies. As word got out among my students that I was officiating at marriage festivities, they began to ask me to do so at their weddings. Consequently, it was my pleasant duty at numerous weddings to say good things about the bride and groom, offer a bit of advice, and lead them through their vows.

Although I had been a guest at many weddings, I had no formal training in the administration of nuptial rituals. I did what it seemed most ministers did, that is, read the words outlined in books of instruction for clergymen performing these rituals. You have all heard them. "Dearly beloved, we are gathered here today to..."

Inasmuch as speaking vows of love and commitment is a very personal thing, I soon became uneasy with this one-ceremony-fits-all approach and abandoned the book and created my own remarks to allow some levity to the occasion, while retaining proper solemnity, and to personalize what I believe is one of the most significant passages of life.

The aspect of the ritual, which bothered me most, was the bit with the rings. It seems that the writers of clerical protocol believed that an explanation of the symbolism of this ritual was essential. I found it hard to believe that, while there may be a lot about love and marriage that seems to defy logic, thinking adults entering in the contract needed instruction about rings. "The ring, an unending circle, represents the unending love confessed here," the book urges the pastor to say. (Suggesting a kind of warranty, perhaps?)

But what happens if the ring breaks? For sixty years I have worn the gold ring Pat gave to me. Last week it cracked; it broke. It now has ends. My inclination is to retire it as a souvenir of sixty delightful years. It has, I say, done its job.

"Not so," argued Pat, as we entered the jewelry shop. They said the warranty had expired and I would have to pay to have it fixed. Pat doesn't want the run to stop just because the ring gave out. She wants whoever is watching to know that the deal is still on.

I reread the clergyman's handbook—no guarantees there.

AUGUST 27

Gran'dogs

The past few weeks we have had a houseguest. Our company is not the ordinary hominoid type. He is an amiable West Highland terrier named Knickers. He is staying at our house while his keepers are moving their household. Grown old, his major activities are eating and sleeping. But he still leaves the impression he thinks (if dogs can do that) that most of the activity about the house has something to do with his welfare, especially the opening of doors. His enthusiasm for a stroll on the leash remains unabated. It has been for us a delightful visit.

I write this largely as comment about how readily a pet invades the ambiance of one's dwelling and too frequently, perhaps, intrudes on thought and conversation. We have had our parade of dogs through our years together. Early on, due to my hunting habits, we kept bird dogs, spaniels, setters, pointers, large dogs whose in-house privileges were limited. Our only in-house dog was Pogo, a delightful little (redundant) Yorkshire terrier who stayed in our house with all the privileges and perquisites pertaining thereto for thirteen years. We have been dogless since Pogo's demise.

Our daughters and their children, who have dogs of which Knickers is one, keep threatening to buy us a puppy. It would be good company they promise. And a lot of work and veterinary bills, I remind myself. While houseguests (grandchildren and gran'dogs alike) are welcome and delightful distractions from the routines of pensioneering, a permanent puppy can't be sent home when it misbehaves. Furthermore, Pat and I provide each other all the constant company we can manage.

AUGUST 28

Symptoms

During the years when my parents were aging and no longer traveled to visit us, our family made an annual trek back to the midwest to visit them. The small idiosyncratic or eccentric behavioral changes attending aging suddenly seemed more noticeable when months passed between visits. And our observations of them surfaced in our conversations as we traveled homeward.

I was raised in a culture where persons exhibiting mildly senile behavior were said to have become "funny." I said to our daughters that I hoped, should I ever become funny, they would tell me. To this they replied, "Oh, Dad, you are already funny."

"But I meant funny as in strange, not funny as in Ha Ha," I said.

"So do we," they said.

While I try not to think a lot about it, I will admit to trying to stay alert to signs that I may, indeed, have succumbed to age-induced funniness. Which isn't funny! So far my daughters haven't said anything, but then they live close by and see me frequently. They may not have noticed.

But today one of them said, "Oh, Dad, you are still funny."

I wonder what she meant.

AUGUST 30

The Book

The deathbed request of a 17th century philosopher is reported to have been, "Bring me the Book." "What book?" he was asked. "What Book? There is only one Book," he replied. I have often heard this story from preachers attempting to establish the pre-eminence of the Bible. My history with the Book goes back at least seven decades to early religious instruction in the Lutheran church. My college undergraduate studies were primarily courses in Biblical Studies. Some years later, preparing sermons to preach to parishioners in a small rural church brought me again to more than casual reading of Holy Script.

No one moves easily among the contours of intellectual thought without a lot of reading. While it is true that one's professional turf often severely restricts one's reading to that of one's specialty, the virtue of liberal education rests on ventures into the literature of all human thought. The fast-moving demanding arena of molecular biology, while intellectually exciting and challenging, unfortunately limited my reading in other domains to mostly recreational excursions.

Fortunately, retirement has afforded me the time to read widely. My stash of things to read these days (and evenings) covers the intellectual landscape—nourishment for the octogenarian mind and soul, I believe. I even read a novel now and then. I am perhaps more liberally informed than when, as a professor, I pretended to be. If it is possible to know more than I need at this stage of life, I may be there. >>>

All of this is preamble to a resolution that I am about to declare about my latter day reading. Why I have neglected regular reading from Pascal's Book I am not sure—not intentionally, I hope. I don't feel any need to be better informed for the imminent reckoning in the sky but, at the risk of being accused by the grandkids of cramming for the final exam, my Bible will move from the library shelf to my bedside stand.

I intend to gravely peruse its pages one more time.

September

SEPTEMBER 1

Lost in Thought

Most of the time what's going on in my mind is such a jumbled potpourri of images, ideas, memories, and apparitions that it's impossible to find the 'me' in all of that disarray. That may be true of everyone, which may account for the tendency of many people to talk all of the time. Talking, I submit, may be a way of pulling something out of that mental gibberish and putting it above the background din. Talking masks the mental ambivalence. Perhaps I should try talking more.

What I am trying to determine is whether the muddle in my mind has always been true or is a function of age or of an idle mind. Could it be that the discs are nearing capacity and all incoming data competing for space stirs the files? The computer gurus insist that nothing gets erased—it only gets written over. How far can one push that analogy?

I think the commotion has always been there, only now I have more time to think about it. One might say, I suppose, that all the stuff that takes up space in one's mental files is no more than a collection of abstractions. But does that mean the notion of self embedded in that mental matrix is less than real? I have a collection of abstractions about professorialism (new word) but, in retrospect, they seem meaningless or of little significance when detached from the 'me' in the mix.

The same is true of all the other notions of self with which I identify—farmer, builder, thinker, preacher, writer, father, husband. Could it be that these mental pictures embody no objective existence? For instance, are all of my cerebral images about farmers colored by my own farming experience devoid of any objectivity?

I think what I am going to do, now that I have time, is look for a composite self-identity in all of the scramble. The procedure on which I am about to embark (in reality an abstraction) might aptly be called compositorialization.

The real "me" has to be in there someplace.

SEPTEMBER 3

What If?

Everyone when reflecting on life, I suppose, encounters dimensions of experience that wishfully might have been different. It must be sad when one is forced to conclude that much of one's life was lacking excitement, fulfillment, or pleasure. Gratefully, my life was never dull, discontented, or devoid of delight. Of course, there were roads not taken which may have been equally delightful.

Lately I have been entertaining some what-ifs, which might have added nuances of flavor or color to the journey. What if, for example, I had had an intimate, life-long, Jewish, African-American, Japanese, or you-name-it friend with a significantly different ethnic or cultural heritage? Even though I am a first generation Norwegian-American, I have always felt and behaved like a white, American Protestant. I suspect I may even have looked like one for the most part.

It's been interesting to speculate about how my story and my outlook on life would be different had I maintained an intimate, enduring relationship with Herb, my Jewish Air Force buddy, or Walt, my Black-American co-worker in a lower-end service job during college, or Sam, my first-generation Italian army pal. I am convinced that my story would read more intriguingly, spiced with color from enduring relationships with those fellows or guys like them.

I liked Herb. He was handsome, pleasant, with a tendency to embellish our antics. I was bewildered because nobody liked him, especially Danny, whose Danish heritage and background was most like mine. Dan liked me but, much to my disquiet, openly derided Herb. Herb was the base photographer who produced my favorite soldier portrait, which we discovered recently perusing old photos. It caused me to wonder what happened to Herb.

Walt and I cleared tables, moved furniture, and mopped floors in a prestigious hotel in Minneapolis. He was strong, quiet, intelligent, and worked hard. Few others on the shift would team with him. Consequently, he and I worked together most of the time. He quietly taught me the hurt inherent in the word *nigger*. The hotel no longer stands, but Walt always surfaces in my reminisces about the old hotel.

Sam was displeased when he caught me rifling his store of Italian sausages sent by his restaurateur parents, but was so delighted that I savored the delicacy that he gave me the entire package. His fantasy was that we would dine together at his Italian family's New Jersey restaurant. It never happened.

Can you tell I have been looking at old army pictures?

SEPTEMBER 4

Two Roads

Two roads diverged in a yellow wood, wrote the poet. He goes on to write about the universal choice encountered by all who meet a fork in the road. He took *the one less traveled by and that made all the difference*, he concludes.

Anyone looking back, as oldsters are prone to do, will recall choices made in their journey. True to expectation I have been reviewing stops in my travels. I suppose this is all pointless, inasmuch as in the business of living one cannot explore both forks in the road at the same time. Nor can one undo the consequences of the choice one did make. I am confident enough to believe I could have been a contender (as the boxer said) in the professions I didn't choose. Ministry or professoriate. Architecture or agriculture. Psychology or biology. Philosophy or science. But being a curious and (I like to think) imaginative guy, I do wonder how the story would read if I had taken *the path with the better claim*, the poet's words.

I learned quickly after retiring that folks generally ask the same three questions. It is as if society has instructed them to inquire of pensioners: Are you busier than ever? Have you been traveling? And if you had it to do all over again, what might you do differently? (I like this one.)

The first two are easy. They are essentially yes or no questions. The third question is the most interesting and prompts me to ponder the poet's predicament. To avoid a lengthy review of all my choices I usually say I made only one significant decision about life's choices, which was to be the best I could be at whatever I chose to do. This effectively stifles further curiosity and I am free to ponder my choices privately.

However, I will confess to whomever may read this how I dealt with options about the final destiny of my trek through the woods. The fork in the forest road seemed to suggest two options: a road to renown or a path to perfection. I chose the latter, *the one less traveled by*.

Little did I know this path has no end.

SEPTEMBER 7

Nobody

I'm nobody. Who are you? Are you nobody too?
Then there's a pair of us — don't tell!
They will banish us you know.   EMILY DICKINSON

Early in my professional life I became aware of publications that catalogued the names and achievements of significant people, the most prestigious of which was Who's Who in America. Because we lived in the West, Who's Who in the West became of some interest to me. I wondered whether I would ever qualify for inclusion among the 'greats.' I also wondered who would nominate me. All the professionals I knew intimately were no more prestigious than I, whose recommendations would be no less dubious than mine.

Then one day I received an official looking letter requesting biographical information about me that might appear in Who's Who in American Science (Western Edition). There were no requests for references that would affirm my qualifications. Later I received a copy of page 482 of the volume in which my short bio appeared among those of 6,749 other wanna-be important people. Included was an invitation to purchase my very own personal copy of the new Who's Who in American Science with my name in it. Slowly I caught on. (Nothing gets by me.) All of this prattle about merit was nothing but exploitation of the egos of persons hungry for recognition. But at least my name was in the big book in whose shadow the Nobodies of American Science live and work.   >>>

Surprised to learn the enterprise still existed, I was reminded of this nonsense by a recent request to update my information as a new edition was being contemplated. I had long forgotten my participation in this self-acclaimed meritocractic elitism. I never did purchase the book, but I confess checking the spelling of my name, which invariably is misspelled stripping me of all renown implied by its inclusion.

I am tempted to produce a volume, which would announce the nobodies of the world. Who's Nobody in America I would call it. I would include all those persons who enter an empty room and the room still seems empty. The guy who answers the doorbell only to be asked, "Is anybody home?" The person whose conversation with a somebody is interrupted by an intruder who didn't notice that he or she was talking to me. Those who bump into a door left to slam shut by a somebody in a hurry. Our nameless next-door-neighbors. The guy who steps back from the urinal in a public restroom unseen by the gadget whose function it is to flush the utility. And all the other invisible persons who frequently hear, "Oh, I didn't see you."

Perhaps we don't really need the volume. We all know who we are.

SEPTEMBER 8

Shadows

At the risk of suggesting there is something shadowy about my life, I admit I like shadows. I have moved about intimately and, I believe, comfortably in the shadows of beautiful, talented, caring, delightful people. My identity has been enhanced immeasurably by association with persons who cast significant and, I might add, persistent shadows.

Evidence of this became apparent at the recent 64th reunion of my high school class. The first three persons I met that afternoon called me Harold. He was my twin brother now deceased 19 years. It is not uncommon for me to be called Harold by people who never knew him. I know of no one ever calling him Howard. Apparently Howards don't leave shadows.

That Harold was eminently more popular than I is without debate. I remember high school girls exclaiming, "There he is!" when they spotted me 20 yards away, only to sigh, "Oh, it's his brother," realizing their mistake and turning away. From the time we were first named we were called Harold and Howard, never Howard and Harold even though I was born first. Always when we were seen together folks would say, "There's Harold and his brother." During teenage years I was invariably identified as Harold Stien's brother. The local hometown newspaper once reporting that I had received a small, but significant scholarship included this footnote: "He is Harold Stien's twin brother." I still have the clipping.   >>>

His was a long shadow.

When I returned home from soldiering in WWII, I met and married a talented young teacher, beautiful in person and spirit, classy in demeanor, gracious. and compassionate. I quickly became and am still invariably introduced as Pat Stien's husband. There's a tall, deep and gentle shadow in which I have been embraced in total delight for sixty years. There's Pat and her husband is a frequent refrain.

The story goes on. I linger in the shadows of two bright, creative, beautiful daughters. As the shadows lengthen, they multiply. I move into a grove of shadows of grandchildren and great-grandchildren.

I know shadows. They are a perquisite of life

SEPTEMBER 10

Unforgettable

This forenoon as Pat and I were leaving the professional studio of a friend, a local businessman, a celebrity of sorts (celebrity with a small c, that is) walked into the room. Our friend, not realizing that we had met the fellow, proceeded to introduce us, whereupon I interrupted to say we had met earlier. It was immediately obvious that the guy had absolutely no recollection of that meeting.

While it is true that we all may not recall some introductions, ours was not what might be said to be an everyday, casual introduction. It occurred at the reception following our granddaughter's wedding ceremony in which I had a hardly insignificant role. Resplendent in my auspicious professional robe, I was hardly inconspicuous, nor could my thoughtful words to the bride and groom be deemed forgettable. After all, I was introduced to the man by the bridegroom's father, yet not a flicker of recognition in the man's eyes.

Perhaps my offense at this reveals more about me than it does about this man's oblivion, but I (like most normal humans) like to be remembered and I am unapologetic for that. It does occur to me, however, that I may be more forgettable than I am willing to acknowledge. I admit being quite shy and unable to indulge in small talk to promote myself. I didn't get gussied up for my granddaughter's wedding so that some tire salesman would notice and remember me later. After all, it was Kyrsten's day. >>>

Apparently I don't do first impressions very well. I am honestly grateful for the ones that went well, above all my introduction to Pat sixty-one years ago this day.

That must have been some introduction!

SEPTEMBER 11

Sandbox

Decades of removing sand and gravel for building and road construction had left a huge crater in a corner of our farmland. The vertical banks of the over-layer of dark fertile farmland gave way to steep slopes of sand and gravel. Scattered tumbleweeds were the only plant residents on the stable floor. A pool of clear water emerged in the deepest part of the crater and provided water for rabbits, foxes, pheasants and other small critters, as well as our draft horses in the drought years. Burrows sheltering the eggs and nestlings of hundreds of cliff swallows perforated the cliffs.

My brothers and I, too young to work in the fields but old enough to be trusted to stay out of mischief, frequently succumbed to the temptation of this huge, off-limit playground. We were warned repeatedly of the dangers of collapsing overburden, falling boulders, and avalanches of gravel.

The interior of the pit largely invisible from the farmstead, however, was an inviting place to bend the rules. We frequently found our way to the forbidden crater, climbed and slid down the sandy slopes, waded in the pool, threw stones from the precipice, troubled the swallow nests, and occasionally ran down a baby cottontail. On one bold, risky escapade we set ablaze a large accumulation of tumble-weeds that had blown into the pit over the winter. No boy had a more delightful sandbox! >>>

Feeling nostalgic today on a trip to Montevideo, Minnesota, my hometown, I drove to the old farmstead wondering what memories I might conjure. The site was only vaguely familiar. Secretly I wanted it to be unchanged, but now 80 years have elapsed since I was born there. Of course, it has changed. The buildings are long gone. The State road that bisected the farmstead is now a high-speed modern highway. The grove of trees that sheltered the house is gone. Our sledding hill has been leveled. It was hauled away to fill sandbags used to manage recent floodwater.

Even the gravel pit is gone. It has been filled with garbage. The site is euphemistically referred to as the County Sanitation Landfill Facility, which translates in my aging mind to City Dump. Somehow I feel sadly diminished, not only by the loss of my favorite boyhood playground but especially by its unflattering fate.

I don't intend to go back.

SEPTEMBER 12

Reunions

People organize reunions for reasons as varied as the circumstances that brought them together in the first place at the same place at some other time now long gone by. Family reunions are perhaps the most common of these gatherings. But at the moment, just having mailed invitations to fifty survivors of the Class of 43 (1943, that is) I am thinking about the most enigmatic of these phenomena—high school class reunions.

Ever wonder what prompts one to attend reunions? As time passes, I have discovered that I can be more honest about why I have been and continue to be drawn to a group of people with whom I moved about for four, formative years in the fighting forties. There were about 110 (now 50) of us interacting intellectually and socially. Socially reticent, I moved mostly on the sidelines. Athletically too small and too late, I watched football games from the bench. I served mostly in scrimmage against the stars. Academically, I was low man on the totem of honor students. But a significant number of us survived not only those years (a war was going on) but also the intervening years, and now propose to meet 64 years later.

Now, with nothing to prove, we might ponder anew the reasons for which we come together one more time. I have heard it said that people gather after:

  10 years to check out the spouses of our high school sweethearts   >>>

- 25 years to talk about our careers
- 45 years to show pictures of our grandkids
- 55 years to compare retirement plans
- 60 years to express gratitude for extra innings
- 65 years to marvel at the wonder of it all.

Some or all of that may be true, but I have concluded what draws us together is a growing appreciation of our common heritage and new affection for old (octogenarian) friends.

And then, maybe, some of us still hope to be noticed.

SEPTEMBER 14

Ancestors

Everyone, I suppose, travels each day by one of those plots of ground where the earthly remains of ancestors have been left and probably in many cases forgotten. Apart from Memorial Day, on which society encourages folks to remember their departed predecessors, I am unaware of any officially sanctioned obligation to visit their resting places.

There is one such place where Pat and I stop—briefly and infrequently, however, given the site is a thousand miles from our home. The little cemetery is a fenced-in patch of prairie in Sparta Township in southwestern McIntosh County in North Dakota. There are no buildings nearby. The little church that once stood by the road, still only a wagon trail, is long gone.

We stop because it is there where Pat's mother, grandparents, great grandparents, several aunts and uncles, and a small number of pioneer neighbors and relatives were interred. It has fallen to Pat to oversee the maintenance of the grounds, which accounts for—in addition to very personal reasons—our annual visits to this place hundreds of miles away. There are for her fond memories of the folks who rest here, especially her grandmother who took her in as a babe. Her influence lovingly lingers large both presently and in memory.

There is history here largely forgotten, I think, by most everyone. One hundred twenty-five years ago her great grandfather Brokofsky gathered pioneer neighbors and relatives in his sod house to worship. That group founded the little Baptist country church that established the cemetery. And out of that beginning comes our heritage in matters of faith and belief.

Those were folks whose days counted.

SEPTEMBER 15

Thanks for the Memories

As these 4th quarter days amass, there are some I can give entirely to thinking; that is, on some days little of significance is going on. Today is one of those days—nothing seems to inspire writing. I am not sufficiently skilled to begin writing with the expectation that some idea, story, or memory will surface and I can take it from there. I have to think before I write, which I submit is a good thing. It precludes writing a bunch of words that don't say anything. Been there, done that. I suppose I could try describing days that don't inspire, but not all days like that are the same. So I have decided to settle in and think. And to focus the endeavor I will ponder this phenomenon of thinking while it is on my mind.

Sometimes I wonder if what goes on in an octogenarian brain differs much from that in younger brains with a reserve of uncommitted neurons. It makes sense that, if arterial function depreciates, neural functions do also. But, as I think about it, I don't think that youthful thought mechanisms differ appreciably, especially if aging has not seriously compromised the neural mechanism of the latter, which may indeed often be true, however. The thought of that possibility ricochets through my thoughts with unwelcome frequency, for example, when I find myself in the bathroom and have to remind myself why I went there.

Anxieties, ambiguities, and ambitions—the content of youthful thought—surely differ from the ambivalences of minds winding down. I have concluded (after thinking about it, of course) that there may be a time when oldsters become too sensitive to the noise of the mental machinery and begin to wonder from where (in the accumulated mass of memory) did this thought come.

I have to think about that. Or perhaps I should just be glad for the memory.

SEPTEMBER 16

Still Driving

Among the fellow worshippers I chatted with after church two weeks ago was Don, whom I had not seen for several weeks. He was not the chipper fellow I was familiar with, less dapper than usual, and suddenly seemed older. "You look a bit pushed down. What's wrong, old timer?" I asked.

"Haven't been doing much other than sitting around," he said. "They won't let me drive anymore. You still driving?" he wanted to know.

"They won't let me drive anymore" is a common refrain among oldsters whose moving about has been curtailed, often under protest, by safety concerned observers. It matters little who they are. The loss of freedom to move oneself beyond the driveway is a major upset not only in the daily routine of living but also tends to be a major hurt to one's mental and emotional sense of well-being.

My conversation with Don occurred the day before our departure on what has long been our annual drive across four states (big western states) to places of significance in our earlier years. The reasons for which we go have changed some, but the distance is the same. The routes we choose are varied. But the roads all take us over the same rivers and mountains. Across prairies. And by the towns we once passed through.

The people we go to see are fewer now. Some of those whom God has privileged us to know and cherish don't live there anymore; some don't live at all. But the drive is still long and challenging given higher speed freeways, more and larger trucks, and scores of cars speeding people to someplace else. There are more boomers in forty-foot motors homes and it seems to me fewer geezers in Buicks.

The drive requires of one skill, alertness, stamina, a lot of luck, and good company. Only on rare occasions have either Pat or I made the drive alone. We arrived home last evening, tired perhaps but not weary; stiff from prolonged immobility; and grateful that the ever watchful 'they' haven't said, "You can't drive anymore."

Yep, we're still driving.

SEPTEMBER 17

Hobby Horses

A former student, now a colleague in the academic department from which I retired, is seriously into horses; that is, horses as hobby. Mike, an energetic, very capable, intelligent young man, does professorial stuff in addition to veterinary medicine. With his passion for learning and compassion for all things living he excels at attending to his students and tending to his horses. His first horse was a huge Clydesdale, a discard he rescued from the Vet School's collection of research animals for whom they no longer had use. He now owns and cares for thirteen of the large critters. I understand Mike's passion for horses.

My boyhood intrigue with my father's huge draft horses on our farm at the twilight of serious horse-powered farming lingers still. My accounts of being sent into the field at the age of ten to harrow the ground with a four-horse hitch of Percherons are legends to our grandkids. We were taught and expected to feed, groom, harness, and drive horses as early as we were physically able. I loved our horses and the day they were sold at auction and led away I hid in the empty barn and sobbed until my twelve-year-old eyes could tear no more. Life, as I had fantasized it, was over.

To Mike my boyhood fascination with horses is quite transparent. He insists I attend the huge regional draft horse show and sale at which he shows and competitively drives his teams. There one sees handsome, perfectly matched, exquisitely groomed, elaborately harnessed six-horse teams of Clydesdales, Percherons, or Belgians expertly driven around the arena. It's nostalgia supreme!

There are dozens of competitions, combinations of hitches, and classes of drivers (children to seniors). Mike has been nagging me to enter a senior competition driving his prize winning 1,800 pound Shire hitched to a two-wheeled sulky. It's tempting. My grandfather had a rig like that except he hitched it to a perky, little, sorrel mare we called Molly. Molly, the last horse our family owned, died while I was away at war.

I haven't agreed to drive Mike's horse and cart. The nostalgia could overwhelm me.

SEPTEMBER 21

The Real Story

It's been said or written somewhere (in fact, it may have been I who said it) that everyone has a story to tell and that all of our stories deserve to be told. I can't vouch for the wisdom or truth of the axiom but I like the essence of it. A life being lived is a story being written. One could go on with the other inferences of the metaphor—a story being told, a story being read, a story forgotten. I think the reminiscences of elderly folks are essentially efforts to reconstruct and preserve their stories. I suspect these reconstructions lack objectivity; nevertheless, I believe they all merit an audience.

I have no reason to believe that the mental scenarios that gyrate in my mind (except for the main characters) differ significantly from those of other eighty-something folks like me. I have to believe the same general threads (yarns?) of thought that hold our stories together are there—albeit quite likely with different spins. On the other hand, however, I suspect that people less introspective than I may not spend a lot of mental or emotional energy thinking about how they came to be who they are. There is a sense in which none of that matters much, inasmuch as none of it can be changed nor can the consequences of any of it be altered.

I can't imagine many curmudgeons worrying about how they got the way they got. Nor can I envision a lot of old-sters trying to change. Too many of us are busy fighting unwelcome changes. Not privileged to see directly into another's mind, I admit wondering what occupies top billing in the minds of my contemporaries. Am I the only one who wonders how the story might read if I had not failed to see the turn-offs that might have led to fame or fortune? I know—it is silly to expend a lot of mental energy inventing what-if scenarios. Too much of that risks confusing the real story, which in most cases is really the more interesting.

I have abandoned my hope to eventually understand it all, which has been said to be the final mental exercise of human minds. It has also been said (and this I didn't say) that the only one who can really tell what life is all about is one who has just died. That is kind of a dead end, is it not?

There is, however, a story about One who did just that, but few there are who believe.

SEPTEMBER 23

No Kings Named Howard

The family genealogist sent me the latest edition of the family pedigree. No surprises in this latest version, but one feature of the tally caught my attention. It was the way certain names have been recycled through the generations. This reuse of names is common practice in family nomenclature. But what caused me no little disquiet was realization that nowhere in the family history does Howard appear until the moniker was assigned to me. Not only that, but while the names of biblically significant or historically great personalities appear frequently in the index (especially in the names of my brothers) no such promise of hope or fame or reminder of family greatness is suggested by the name Howard.

All four of my brothers were tagged with names of greatness or names of significant family forebears:

My twin brother Harold was named after the famous Viking King Harald, as well as both a paternal and maternal uncle.

Brother Richard John was given the name of two Uncle Johns as well the title of King Richard. One might also wonder whether thoughts of the Apostle John lingered there.

Donald was not so lucky, or perhaps luckier with no traditions to sustain. He did have an older Cousin Donald and there was a paternal uncle named Reinert, Don's second name.

Raymond had a great second name, a name I silently coveted for years. He was Raymond Peder, a Scandinavian rendition of Peter. His appearance apparently inspired the best in my folks naming endeavors. There was Grandfather Hans Peder, an Uncle Peder, and, of course, Peter the Great, as well as the famous Apostle Peter.

I often wondered what my parents had in mind when they tagged me Howard. True, they were new at the business of assigning names. I was the first of the five brothers. But they should have known there are no kings named Howard.

Neither are there any saints named Howard, unless ...

SEPTEMBER 24

Stages of Life

Persons among the senior citizen ranks, like me, are frequently greeted (especially by folks we have not seen recently) with the words, "Wow, you look great!" I believe that most folks are being polite. One would hardly say to anyone, "You look terrible." I like it when folks say flattering things to me and usually tend to believe them. But I suspect that the expression is more a ritual than an honest assessment of my countenance. I think it is more likely to be recognition (or reminder) of my stage in life. Scholars who ponder life's stages use words like juvenescence, pubescence, adolescence, middlescence, senescence, and sometimes obsolescence to name the phases through which persons progress. But most folks don't know those words. And who would say to an octogenarian, "Wow, you model senescence well!" when they probably mean, "Wow, for an old guy you sure look good."

It was homecoming weekend at our college and I moseyed onto campus to perchance encounter some of my favorite former students. I was pleased, surprised, and a bit troubled by their greetings, which went something like this: "Wow, you look great—you haven't changed a bit." And that from folks whom I hadn't seen for twenty-five years. I want to say "Don't you see that the gorgeous salt and pepper hair has turned to monotonous white? Can't you see the added twenty pounds—one pound for each of the ensuing

20 years—the slight bend in the once-stately upright posture, the weathered face, the less than quick recall of names and events, the countenance of accumulative age inspired wisdom? But I don't. I am content just to look great.

I do, however, wonder why these students, whom I thought I had taught to be objective observers of things and events biological, have lost sight of the constant progressive changes confronting all living things, including aging professors.

There even is a word for it—Gerontomorphosis.

SEPTEMBER 25

Some New Thing

When one writes or talks of something new, it is invariably in reference or relative to something old. Things, people, and ideas all eventually get old. If anything new occurs in an aging body it is likely to be some new hurt or limitation giving credence to the thought that new may not always be better. There is some dissonance in the idea of a new prescription for an old guy.

"We can fix that," the doctor said. "We can give you a new hip. That will eliminate your uneven step." I had sought his counsel about an annoying hobble that had been developing in my walk and seemed to suggest a flaw to some observers. I had exhausted my store of clever replies to insensitive questions: Have you noticed you are limping? When did you begin to walk like that? "Thanks for noticing," I would say, or "I am sorry. I didn't mean to do that." But it wasn't the discomfort from the condition that motivated my consultation with the doc as much as it was the innuendo from friends that I was impaired, a possibility quite bothersome to this stoic Norwegian

The exchange of the old for the new went surprising well. It didn't hurt all that much; I regained my balanced stride; and people again became indifferent to my gait. I had been a dedicated runner and was warned to abstain from that because of the potential to harm the prosthesis.   >>>

I adjusted to that limitation and got on quite well with this new thing. Until I began to be disquieted by the realization that I was now flawed in a different way—however, obvious to no one but the X-ray machine and me. Whereas I had been pure 100% Norwegian, I have been reduced by whatever part of me is now cobalt, chromium, and titanium.

I can't imagine the dissonance had it been Swedish steel.

SEPTEMBER 27

Postscripts

Recent news reported the passing of Naquib Mahjouz, Nobel Laureate Egyptian writer, little known except by the most literary elite. I admit I had not known of him and his writing before I read the piece—essentially an obituary—in one of the weekly news magazines. I was surprisingly impressed by the language with which the reporter described the man. The tribute portrayed him as a person of incredible moral clarity, immense wisdom, gentility of spirit, and unyielding tolerance. I have no reason to question the validity of the accolades. It seems that he was, indeed, an exceptional person.

My incorrigible cynicism causes me to read most postscripts about people passed on with a bit of suspicion that some honest inflation usually creeps into the account. It would be preferable if all of us lived our lives so that the folks to whom it falls to write of our departure could do so without jeopardizing their commitment to truth. But, after all, we are all flawed in some way and our survivors must do the best with what we give them.

The characteristics attributed to the writer are enviable. While I certainly would like something like that written about me, I know it's highly unlikely. Why should I, who went about my business only minimally concerned about what others thought, now wonder what my after-words would say? I am inclined to think it doesn't matter.

So why am I still trying?

SEPTEMBER 28

Making Lists

Some folks, Pat is one of them, begin their day by making a list of tasks that they intend to accomplish before nightfall. I never made lists, at least not written lists. I anticipated and attempted to avoid the nagging that might ensue from an unfinished list. But recently in these days of repose, it appears I have begun to dabble with lists. These are lists that reside quietly in my mind and, as long as my memory remains reliable, they serve largely to organize the musings that surface in my consciousness while I go about doing the things on Pat's list.

My lists are private—that is, I don't talk much about them, inasmuch as they are not the sorts of lists that occur readily to normal folks. In fact, I am not always aware of their existence. I chatted briefly with a friend after church and in the small talk typical of chance social encounters I inquired of his well being. He, an unusually cheerful person, replied, "I am fine. Life couldn't be better." To this I said, "Then I will put you on my list of People Not to Worry About."

I think he was too surprised to be amused. "Wow, I didn't know anyone made lists like that," he said. I was surprised too. I didn't know the list existed either until that moment. It's a good list and with all the happy, contented folks around it certainly eases the clutter in my mind, now that I think about it. That experience caused me to wonder briefly whether there are other odd indexes mounting in my mind.   >>>

Pat and I were making our way through Wyoming last week. The landscape was unusually green, exceptionally beautiful, and my mind was flooded with wistful reminiscences about our sojourn in Wyoming four decades ago. Basking in the nostalgia, I reported to Pat that I was going to put our time at the University of Wyoming on my list of Better Things We Have Done. Every oldster should have a list like that.

I have begun to listen to myself more carefully, perchance to learn of other lists I am making.

SEPTEMBER 29

Rainy Day

Today is a rainy day. Even though that is what is going on, I cannot bring myself to write, "It's raining outside today." For one thing it seldom rains inside at our house. But more troubling is the reference to Nature as *it*. I have become uncomfortable referring to Nature in all of its created grandeur and power as *it*. To do so is, of course, correct grammatically and everybody I am sure understands the idiom. *It* is a powerful word. It can be used to denote anything and everything. Traditionally, meaning is determined by the last preceding noun. Not so in the simple announcement, "It's raining." *It* in this case is whatever one wants it to be.

I don't know what (except, perhaps, the fact that it is indeed raining) occasioned this analysis of the way one should structure sentences including the word *it* when all I intended to write was, "Rain is falling today."

Because it is raining (or preferably because rain is indeed falling) and I can't get on with my out-of-the-house activities, I have time to ponder whether falling rain is inherently redundant. It seems to me that the word rain implies falling, that is, that rain cannot not fall.

The way I see it (there's that word again) water fallen or falling from the sky is rain and, according to Holy Script, falls on the just and the unjust.

It is true. If we go outdoors on a rainy day, invariably both Pat and I get wet.

October

OCTOBER 1

Nothing to Say

An elderly acquaintance has become exceptionally quiet to the extent that his wife complained that he simply doesn't talk anymore. When asked why he doesn't talk he replied, "I don't have anything to say." While I have long insisted that to refrain from talking when one had nothing to say was a virtue, this was an intelligent, sociable, successful, enlightened professional with whom conversation was always pleasant. Could it be that thoughtful persons reach a stage in the aging progression when it occurs to them all they have to say has been said, I wondered, or that no new thing to say has surfaced in their minds?

During my professionally active years I responded quite eagerly to invitations to speak; that is, to make a speech. It seldom entered my mind that I may have nothing of significance to say. Now I recoil at the thought of making a speech. The possibility that I may have nothing new to say looms large. Who among us has not sat through countless speeches where the speaker really had nothing to say, but proceeded to talk nevertheless.

This, however, is not about making speeches. It's about making conversation, an essential feature of human interaction. Except that aging may enhance wisdom, I am not yet convinced oldsters can legitimately claim that aging naturally dampens ones inclination to talk. It seems to me that old friends, who tended to talk too much, still do and thoughtful folks still talk less. I have always thought of myself, albeit humbly, as a quiet guy disinclined to fight my way into a conversation being dominated by folks unaccustomed to listening.

One may have to stop talking to hear what the silent ones are saying.

OCTOBER 3

Soot is OK

Today I cleaned the chimneys. Cleaning chimneys was romanticized in the popular film Mary Poppins. The chimney sweep in that movie was so inspired by his work that he danced on the roof and sang, *I like what I does and I does what I like.* I realize that in the movies anything is possible, but I am here to tell you that in the real world of soot, smoke, and ashes there is nothing glamorous about cleaning chimneys. Nothing about it could cause me or any psychologically sound person (not even with Mary Poppins standing by) to dance or sing.

Being on the roof entails some risk but reasonable precaution minimizes that. It's the soot that cannot be avoided. And it is the accumulation thereof that demands attention. Containing the stuff scraped from the chimney surfaces and sequestering it is the major challenge. It is the grimiest, elusive substance imaginable and blacker than a raven's wing. I never did master handling soot. Perhaps the professionals can and that is why they sing.

Soot is the blackest stuff conceivable and clings to one hands with unmatched tenacity. (Yes, I know about gloves.) My hands, my face, my clothes, everything nearby invariably become blacker than sin. But it is, along with other kinds of dirt, the sort that eventually will wash away.

When I was a boy and would resist barnyard chores, such as cleaning the cow barn, chicken coop or pigpen, my mother would say, "Dirt that will wash off won't hurt. It is dirt that you can't wash off that will."

Soot may be OK, but I am still not inclined to dance and sing about it.

OCTOBER 5

Final Steps

The largest list of synonyms devoted to the understanding of a single word in my dictionary is that used to delimit the meaning of the word *step*. The word *step* literally denotes the measure of distance traveled in each of the repeated movements of one's legs while walking. The word *steps* has, of course, invaded figurative discourse dealing with increments; for example, phases, stages, units, parts, and pieces. But I am thinking about literal steps, especially the number of steps in any from-here-to-there space, and the number of steps in a given time; such as, steps in a lifetime. An appropriate concern for one in the exit lane.

There is a notion bantered about in zoology that there is a fixed, life-time number of heart beats allotted to individuals of all species and that number is independent of the rate at which the heart beats. Furthermore, the argument insists that number is generally the same for all creatures large and small. For example, a hummingbird heart beats 800 times per minute while an elephant heart beats eight times per minute, but it's all over when each of them has spent the same allotted number of ticks.

I won't vouch for either the validity or acceptance of the theory, but it can generate interesting after-dinner conversation. It has occurred to me to wonder, however, whether the same thing may be said of the number of steps allotted to a lifetime. There is an immense difference in the number of steps around the block required by our neighbor and by her dachshund puppy. I worry that he may exhaust his quota early. One might also wonder how the number of legs factors into the count. Consider the poor centipede.

All of this came to mind as I was contemplating the increase in the number of times oldsters are admonished to watch their step. I don't know how many steps there are in a lifetime. It must be predetermined, given the constant caution about steps. My mother used to say, "Watch your step, young man." My rancher friend says when showing me his cattle, "Watch your step." Now people say, "Watch your step, old man." And then the notion of final steps does creep into the minds of thoughtful oldsters. I try not to think about it.

But it does behoove one to keep looking down.

OCTOBER 7

Intellectual Grazing

With characteristic cynicism I read a recent Time Magazine article entitled Growing Up Grieving. My tendency to read pieces like that with some objectivity takes me beyond the facts about the actual cases to the sociology of the studies. I am certain that the facts about losses experienced by 9/11 children too young to comprehend are very real. My disquiet about it all stems from the apparent need of 'scholar-researchers' to see this group of unfortunate, suffering individuals as forage for intellectual grazing. One wonders whether apart from providing grist for sociological studies this continued preoccupation serves any purpose. Thinking persons are not unaware of the anguish of the families most intimately touched by this horror, but to what extent does the knowledge obligate us to intellectualize about it?

Furthermore, does the fact that 3,000 children lost a parent all at the same time infer any special status to this group? Are their losses any more grave than the boy whose father was killed in this unnecessary war? I suppose somewhere someone is studying the consequences to a child of having lost a parent in battle, but that study will not have the academic advantage of presenting a neatly packaged group of subjects. The grass is less green there.

I am convinced that little of any value accrues to the children from being the subjects of academic studies that appear more descriptive than prescriptive, that is, what to do about it.

The studies do, however, as demonstrated by the fact that I did indeed read this piece, call our attention again to a group of people whose lives have been tragically disrupted. It should raise our level of compassion and remind us of our human tendency to become indifferent to tragedy or misfortune that doesn't touch us, but that is seldom the stated intent or motivation of this kind of study. Is it to submit one more entry into one's scholarly resume?

I entered retirement with the expectation that some time away from the arena of academic or intellectual pretense would purge me of cynicism about why scholars write.

It seems the cynic in me remains unpurged.

OCTOBER 10

Unlikely Spots

The sign is gone. Hard to miss—it was attached to a replica of a pioneer covered wagon that stood on a hillside near the Interstate in Montana. In bold letters it announced SPOTTED ASS RANCH. Another identical sign 15 miles further down the same highway marked the limits of this large ranch. Usually a dozen burros would be seen feeding or lounging nearby. Their coats were indeed spotted, an unusual coloration on these usually drab but fascinating critters. On our many jaunts across Montana we watched attentively for them, which invariably generated interesting conversation, sometimes about the fantasy of owning one of these unusual animals and what it might be like to have a spotted ass.

Donkeys aside, the word ass conjures a curious mixture of reminisces about my experiences with words. The word ass has a curious range of meaning. My dictionary lists three: an animal resembling a small horse with long ears; an offensive term for an unintelligent, thoughtless, or ridiculous person; an obscene term for the human derriére.

I can still recall the dissonance in my childhood mind over the off-limits of the word ass in polite company and the acceptance of the word in the reading of Scripture in church, which made references to Jesus' mode of transport on Palm Sunday. Calling an unmanageable sibling an ass was not simply naughty; it was unforgivable, worthy of Mother's reprehension. And using the common vulgar invitation to kiss one's derriére should absolutely never be uttered on the playground, much less in the house. It was OK to say ass in Sunday school, however.

Vulgarity has become quite acceptable these days and one hears the word on television, films, and sees it regularly in print. (Ironically, newer translations of the Bible call donkeys *donkeys*.)

What has all this to do with burros in Montana? Nothing I suppose, except that with the SPOTTED ASS RANCH no longer in business, where can one go to get a spotted ass?

Try the tattoo parlor?

OCTOBER 11

No Song to Sing

In all of the places we have lived the advent of spring was never more welcome than on the North Dakota farm. One of the many delightful aspects of spring on the prairie was the arrival of meadowlarks with their melodious, six-syllable songs. One spring the larks arrived early before the cold winds abated. They huddled in the shelter of tufts of last summer's vegetation, but they didn't sing. Uncle David, a veteran of prairie springtime, predicted that the birds would sing when they had something to sing about. "Now they have nothing to sing about," he said.

For most of our sixty years together there has been a piano in our living room. Our daughters practiced their lessons there and Pat maintained her touch. Our family sang a lot around the various pianos that stood in our parlors, especially at gatherings of the clan. We sang in church, in the car on the road. I sang in the shower and in the field accompanied by the rhythm of the tractor engine.

We don't sing much anymore. I am hesitant to conclude that in our hearts there is no song. It could be that contemporary popular music these days is mostly unsingable—yelling and screaming with unimaginably inane lyrics. The new songs don't inspire us. But the old favorite songs, popular songs of decades gone by, the old favorite hymns and folk songs are still here to be sung. The piano is still in its corner. The tractor is gone, but the shower and the car are still here.

The reasons for which we sang still exist. But the voices that once moved us to sing are softer now, our notes less true. Could it be the season?

Now that I think about it, the meadowlarks didn't sing much in autumn either.

OCTOBER 12

Ticks

Most well adjusted oldsters find things to keep themselves mentally alert. It has been said that a mind, even an aged mind, is a terrible thing to waste. Professors, retired and otherwise, are instinctively drawn to the conclusion that the words *professor* and *writer* are synonymous. I tend to believe that is true, more so about me perhaps than for other professors, who have demonstrated by writing that it may not be. At the risk of that becoming my fate, I persist in my writing endeavors for reasons about which I am still uncertain. Whatever the outcome, I am convinced that the activity clears the mind.

Like all writers, accomplished or self-proclaimed, I am pleased when someone reads my stuff or even asks if I am writing anything these days. Pat reminds me occasionally that I may be too quick to hand something to read to anyone who asks. She points out that they didn't ask to read, only whether I had written something. But I still leave some of my stuff in prominent places on the coffee table just in case the curiosity is sincere.

One, however, must be prepared for the comments that may result from someone having read one's words. Actually, I am interested in comments about the sophistication, creativity, cleverness, or uniqueness of my writing than I am about the content. That is not to say I am indifferent to what readers think about my stories, some of which I think are pretty good. 　　　　　　　　　　　　　　　　　　＞＞＞

On a recent holiday with two very good friends, I brought along a manuscript of some recent palaver I had been writing with the excuse that I was going to do some editing. I left it in plain view purposely, if perchance we ran out of conversation or things to read they might pick it up. It worked. It was in a bright red folder, hard to miss. Both Bob and Nancy read it with visibly genuine interest. I was pleased for their comments and affirmation.

But I learned something I didn't know, which is always good even for aspiring octogenarian writers. Most writing, good or bad, eventually reveals something about the author. Nancy's kind remarks included the surprising observation, "Now I know what makes Howard tick!"

I had no idea I ticked.

OCTOBER 13

It's in the Telling

Our late autumn days are still delightfully Indian Summer-like, weather for which Spokane is noted. Pat and I drove leisurely to Sandpoint yesterday. We did our usual Coldwater Creek caper and early-bird dinner at Swan's Landing. We had our 6-month visit with Dr. Clode earlier in the day. If there is (and I think there may be) some sort of natural deterioration calendar, we may be a bit behind schedule for which we are grateful. That may have been what motivated us to impulsively jump (scratch jump—we do less of that these days) climb into the car and go for a drive. We may have been looking for a way to spend some of the $300 we saved by buying drugs in Canada. On the other hand, that had already been spent. We did buy a new car. But I digress. Our holiday drive to Idaho was an intentional diversion from activity the doc is prescribing. "Have you established a daily walk schedule?" he asked.

I am trying to maintain my daily trek up the hills in the power line right-of-way. Frequently, as I walk I amuse myself with words like assembling collections of synonyms. Did you know there are nearly thirty words that in someway describe the act of walking? Stroll. stride, amble, saunter, skip, prance, trot, jog, shuffle, hobble, plod, traipse, etcetera, etcetera.

These words come to mind as I make my way along my route under the power line right-of-way. The change in elevation on this route is brutal. I marvel at the ease with which the young guys effortlessly truck on by me. (Trucking—there's another version.)

I discovered a new word to describe the manner in which I walk up that rise. I trudge (truj v.t. to walk laboriously) up the hill. Is there such a word as trudgery? I think there ought to be. It wouldn't make the trek any easier, but one would know what one was facing. Trudgery is akin to drudgery, except it is more precise.

And then there is fudgery; that is, telling the doctor you trudge every day.

OCTOBER 15

Now You Know

Momentarily disavowing my resolve not to participate with my fellow pensioners in the practice of reviewing recent medical histories, my penchant for privacy notwithstanding, I decided to amuse myself with a little tomfoolery while profaning some of my very personal medical past. This could also serve as a comment about the medical profession's proclivity to use big words for small operations, while at the same time practicing my predilection to indulge in a bit of alliteration.

Debridement as defined in my medical dictionary: *de-bride´ ment (de-breed´ mahn´ ; de-breed´ ment) [F.] In surgery, the removal of foreign material or devitalized tissue from a wound or injury that fails to heal.* The word has as its root in the word debris (pronounced day-bree´) derived from the old French word debrissiér, which only coincidentally sounds like another French word, derriére. I don't mean to suggest that there is any etymological relationship between the words debris, debridement, and derriére, but they all come together this afternoon when Dr. White will disinter the devitalized cells and repair the ugly hole (a lingering consequence of an earlier surgery) from the superficial tissues overlying the lateral aspect of my derriére.

It's highly unlikely, but should you encounter an occasion to talk about this, you now know how to do it with appropriate alliterative alacrity.

OCTOBER 16

'Rellies' in the Park

One city block away from our daughter's house in St. Paul there is a large, popular, beautiful, well-kept city park. One of its major attractions is the zoo, a relatively small but creatively displayed collection of large animals—the species that fascinate small children and aging zoologists like me. Through the years I made numerous visits to the zoo, usually in the custody of grandchildren who indulged my fascination with the marvelous creatures sequestered there, while they patiently waited for their turn on the carnival rides in the adjacent amusement park.

In recent years with the grandchildren grown and gone (although I did accompany two great grandchildren there last summer) my recent trips to this favorite zoo have been alone, which afforded me time to leisurely observe the animals and ponder the Creator's intention with these exquisite critters. I marvel at the unique differences yet subtle similarities in the design of these creatures, which I professionally have come to see as variations on a theme. I am especially intrigued by what are apes to most people but primates to me—so much like yet so unlike us. With a bit of evolutionary bias I have come to think of the chimps, orangutans, and gorillas as distant relatives.

My family chides me about my lingering at the primate exhibit. "The monkey house," they say—fearful, I suspect, that I may begin to take this relative thing too seriously.

"Been spending time with the 'rellies' in the park again?" they ask.

Today, while taking a break from loading the U-Haul (Suzanne and Terry are moving away from Saint Paul), I sauntered to the zoo to have one last look at the 'rellies' there. To say goodbye, I suppose. They all, especially the orangs (my favorites) seemed quite indifferent. I didn't stay long.

Being dissed by relatives no matter how distant is not a pleasant thing.

OCTOBER 18

Moving On

Today, after several days of intense activity both emotional and physical, Suzanne, Terry and I set out from Minnesota to Spokane with two drive-yourself trucks. The trucks were stuffed with the accumulation of their worldly, material goods—personal fixings, as the weigh station guy referred to the loads. Our challenge was to get the stuff across North Dakota prairies and over Montana's endless grasslands and immense Rocky Mountains before the snows came to ice the mountain passes.

This would be my fourth such journey carrying (a southern expression meaning transporting) personal fixings over this same route. Pat and I moved our family's stuff (there is no better word to denote the accumulation of things we can't bring ourselves to leave behind) over this exact route forty-one years earlier. While that trip took us through the same cities, it wasn't exactly the same route in that the interstate highway through this area was not finished at that time. Much of the course then was on narrow, two-lane, circuitous roads. While challenging at times, it relieved some of the boredom of modern multi-lane freeways. Today there are no stoplights on the entire route. One can travel from St. Paul to Spokane without stopping, except for fuel, food, rest, and other comforts one might choose. Our trip, while not without stress, was successful. The stuff is safely stashed in storage spaces, decisions about its final destiny still pending. >>>

Much can be said or written about this 1,500-mile journey, which I likely will do someday. I have traveled the distance by train, truck, plane, automobile, and some of it by bicycle more times than I am willing to admit. And invariably each departure was preceded by deliberations about what I should carry with me. But this is not about the trip per se. It's this thing we have about things that comes into focus when we make a major move. Most oldsters enter the exit lane encumbered to varying degrees with stuff, some of which has moved with them throughout the journey. I wonder how many of us deal with the reality that there are no baggage claims at the end this trip.

One can only hope one's carry-on stuff is in order.

OCTOBER 19

Delinquent

While driving around the outskirts of our town, we happened by the first house into which we moved when we came to the city forty-two years ago. The house, a modest 1965 model, looks pretty much as it did when we lived there. The community is essentially unchanged except for forty years of growth on the Ponderosa pine trees. The house next door, which was built during the early years of our tenure there, was also unchanged. It was that house, not our former dwelling, that not very gently stirred my memories.

A young couple lived in a troubled, tumultuous relationship there. The father, a professional man, was there sporadically and eventually not at all. The petite, pretty, young mother continued to live there with a handsome small boy, whose name was Danny, I believe. Danny was often left alone and frequently wandered onto our driveway to chat and follow me around as I tended to outdoor chores. He seemed to think of our encounter as play. One day when I came home from the college, Pat announced that Danny had come to our door asking, "Can Dr. Stien come out to play?" Being a bit amused at his request, I dismissed that as his father's job. I was too busy with personal tasks and, of course, my studies.

Danny never asked me to play again. He grew to become a troubled adolescent, went from mischief to misdemeanor and juvenile delinquent in the parlance of the time. Later, after we had moved from the neighborhood, I read in the local newspaper that Danny was on his way to prison convicted of serious crime. Whether my going out to play with him may have deterred him from serious delinquency, I cannot know. But the reminder that I was too busy to play with a troubled, lonely, little boy not only haunts me, it hurts.

I have tried to forget my delinquency, but sight of the house won't let me.

OCTOBER 21

Outings

In this counting of days in the ninth decade, I have often used extra innings to denote the days or years beyond the Biblical fourscore allotment. I haven't given much thought to the effectiveness of the analogy, but watching the agonizingly slow pace of World Series baseball does cause one to wonder about the jargon of the game. I have wondered, for instance, whether the interminable time between innings might be called outings. Outings, a legitimate antonym of innings, have no play in the game of baseball, which has outs but strangely no outings. I think if the game did indeed have outings it may appeal more to thinking people.

I think of outings as sort of mini-excursions characterized by fun, enjoyment, nostalgia, pleasurable activity, perhaps on the margins of the ordinary—like picking chokecherries with my daughter. I walked by the chokecherry tree, which we stripped of its fruit last year, and began to reminisce about that delightful Saturday afternoon. That was an outing in my best sense of the word.

Then I thought of other outings. We scrambled over the junked cars abandoned in a gravel pit in suburban Laramie harvesting tail light glass for an art project. That was an outing. Or duck hunting on the North Dakota ponds; studying mummies at the Los Angles Museum of Natural History; skating in Loring Park while Mom was at work; or scrutinizing art at the Walker Art Institute. Outings squeezed between the innings of life. >>>

Now there's an analogy that needs refinement, but it occurs to me that my use of extra innings to indicate that one is still in the game may need to be adjusted to make room for some excitement between innings.

Bonus years notwithstanding, there ought to be some outings.

OCTOBER 23

Soulful Reserves

It was a long time ago when I first submitted my doctoral thesis to my mentor for critique. His comment was, "This is good writing, but the style is too literary for good scientific reporting. Now go through it and get the fat out. There is too much you in it." I had assumed too much me was not necessarily a bad thing and was able to convince the other advisors. So the thesis remains much like my original draft. I still like it. I happened onto it recently when sorting books to give to our daughters, a common retirement activity.

All of which brings me to thoughts about my mentor, a good guy about whom pleasant thoughts come readily. His expressions were provocative and to the point. It is remarkable how indelibly some of them were etched into my recollections of those heady days of academic quest.

When I completed the program I was not only awarded the degree, I was complimented by an invitation to join the university faculty and flattered because university policy generally precluded hiring recent graduates. When I told Garth I intended to decline the prestigious invitation and seek my intellectual and academic fortune at small private liberal arts colleges, surprisingly he said, "Yes, I think you should. Go and get the fat out of your soul and then come back." He was a thoughtful guy and frequently used the word fat to indicate excess in any context. But fat souls—what did that mean? Come back and do science purged of notions about non-material realities was the innuendo I heard.

Often throughout 40 years in the midst of scholars, some of whom my mentor would have judged too fat in soul, I have pondered the state of my soul and wondered whether any purging was, indeed, occurring. My education in the precepts of biology had convinced me that some fat was a good thing. Fat is a stored reserve, energy for times of scarcity. Is a bit of fat in the reserves stored in one's soul necessarily a bad thing? Contrary to my prof's notion that fat in the soul should be rendered, I am convinced that a bit of fat in one's soul is good for life.

That's where the flavor is.

OCTOBER 27

Old or Older

A professorial colleague died last week. He was one of the profs on the faculty of Migh College when we arrived here forty years ago. The group is getting smaller and doing so more quickly it seems. There are six of them still living, all but one over 80. Professorializing (I love that word) must be good for the body; I hope it is also good for the soul. But the demise of contemporary colleagues is a bleak reminder that I, too, am getting older.

Does it make sense to say I am getting older? Everyone is getting older, even those young in mind and soul and body. Getting old, however, is something quite different. While the difference is probably semantic, one experiences old quite differently than simply being older. I prefer to think of myself still in the getting older category where the changes are more subtle and easier to ignore. I think awareness of the difference is the only significant difference. Perhaps not being occupied with earning a living leaves one more headspace to devote to other tasks—like staying healthy and contending with evidence that health, in fact, life is precarious.

One may be casual about getting older but the evidence that one is progressing into the other category emerges more forcefully into one's consciousness and sometimes is difficult to discount—like the passing of friends gotten old. I prefer 'older man' to 'old man.'

The difference is innuendo.

OCTOBER 29

Hanging

In polite, casual, personal discourse we humans have adopted language customs to ease conversation. After preliminary salutations like Hello, Hi, Hey, and Good Morning, one can expect to hear inquiries about one's health and other aspects of one's welfare. Or folks will want to know about one's daily routines. Queries like: How are you? How's it going? What's up? and Whatcha been doin'? are meant to be ceremonial rather than literal questions. These, unfortunately, are too often misunderstood to be the latter. One receives mundane details about health, travel, misfortune, and grandchildren—making one wish one hadn't asked.

Happily, responses to these conversation-starting inquiries have likewise been abridged. "I'm fine" or "I'm well" or "I'm good" are common replies to "How the heck are you?" I do often wonder, however, whether the responses indicate one's moral condition or one's physical well being.

Today is one of those days that encourage doing nothing. Honest curiosity, I suppose, constrains some folks to ask us oldsters, whose activity isn't defined by career or profession, "What are you doing these days?" or "What are you up to?" My settled abridged reply is "Just hanging out." Sometimes I use the adolescent version "Just hanging." I don't often reflect on why I say that or justify the response. It could be that I don't wish to be judged about my idleness or lack of productivity in someone's scheme of accountability. Or it could be a way to avoid discomforting folks with more information than they really wanted or needed to know.

I marvel at my sensitivity, but I worry that it leaves some folks hanging.

OCTOBER 30

Ethnic Eccentricity

Returning from a trip to Minnesota (the Land of Lakes, loons, lefse, and lutefisk) daughter Beth brought me a bumper sticker that read LEGALIZE LUTEFISK. If you are an adult who doesn't know what lutefisk is, it is best you don't ask. Unless you ask a true believer, it is highly improbable that you will receive an objective or honest description of this culinary delight. In my experience folks who have had the most minimal exposure to lutefisk are the loudest in their negative and tasteless accounts of the delicacy.

While I object to the claim by some that to really enjoy lutefisk one has to have been weaned on the stuff, I can't remember not having this delectable dish on the festive days of winter. (By the way, it is not true that pioneer Norwegian Lutheran immigrants used coffee to baptize their infants.) Lutefisk began to appear on our table at Thanksgiving and frequently thereafter through Christmas, exquisitely prepared by my Danish mother. My credentials as a connoisseur border on professional.

One might argue that honest connoisseurs of lutefisk are eccentric. I have even heard the claim that Norwegians are by definition eccentric and their happy consumption of lutefisk is the primary evidence thereof. We are no more or less eccentric than others who cherish such ethnic dietary peculiarities as sauerkraut, spaghetti, borscht, kidney pie, and tripe. However, none of these delectably debatable dishes suffers the abuse of lutefisk from those with limited gustatory sophistication.

So I am eccentric, which doesn't offend me. What does trouble me, however, is my observation that in this age of sensitivity few people are bothered that lutefisk aficionados remain outside the sheltering bounds of political correctness.

The Sons of Norway will soon feature their seasonal lutefisk dinners. As the Minnesotans would say, "Want to go with?"

November

NOVEMBER 1

A Reminder

During our professional tenure Pat and I were flattered by invitations from many of our students to attend their weddings. In fact, I was pleased to be asked to officiate at several student weddings. After observing scores of weddings I suspect that few of the youngsters who respond to the clergyman's "Repeat after me" give more than ritual attention to what the vows actually say. They are too deeply engaged with the now.

They agree to faithfully weather misfortune as well as good fortune or illness along with wellness. Most who promise think that's how life shakes down, I am guessing, and I accept that. In fact, wedding vows are not only promises but also predictions about what one should expect. Traditionally the vows end with a reminder that the promises will expire. That's the 'until death do us part' part.

That matrimony is a terminal arrangement doesn't readily occur to normal persons in the context of a happy wedding celebration. After all, this is a time of beginnings. Unfortunately, not every marriage is a 'happily ever after' affair. But that is not what this is about. Rather, it is about those that are.

Last week Pat and I encountered one of those scary, later-in-life occasions when the final words of our wedding vows stir in the subconscious. You all know the routine—paramedics, emergency room, urgent procedures, doctor's report, sighs of relief, prayers of gratitude, and reunion with anxious family folks. These are not moments when thoughts turn first to ancient promises, but rather to the journey itself.

After the threat has been subdued and the patient is resting, one leaves the hospital, goes home alone to ponder it all in a place strangely cold, big, and empty.

A not-so-gentle reminder about those final words.

NOVEMBER 3

Untold Story

The lives of families, not unlike the lives of individuals, are stories being told. I have often wondered how a story about my parents and siblings would read. To write that story is one of my unfinished aspirations. I actually began the story several times, but the writing never got traction, as contemporary jargon would say. It seemed the narrative wanted to move in the direction of the antics of the brothers.

My twin brother and I were the first of the pentad of sons, followed quickly within five years by Dick, Don, and Ray born to Ole and Dagmar, our Scandinavian immigrant parents. Because our heights were somewhat inversely proportional to our ages, we were all about the same size for a few years. With a strong family resemblance in our teenage years we were perceived more as a gang than as individuals. We were the Stien boys, more often Ole Stien's boys, shortened on occasion to OSBs. Folks would say, "That bunch of guys should go places." It was even suggested now and then what one of those places might be.

The band of brothers dispersed almost as quickly as it formed. Life for large families was not easy in the thirties. As soon as we were old enough to work and earn money to support the family, Harold and I, and then Dick, were hired out as farmhands during summers and non-school days. World War II spread us out further. Our lives moved in different directions and the plot of our mutual story dissolved.

I did settle on the title for this unwritten book. When I do write it, I will call it Dagmar and The Sons of Ole.

Now there's a novel idea.

NOVEMBER 4

On Being Tall

Today marks the start of serious contention on the country's basketball courts. The intense courting of tall, young athletes is over for now and the season with incredible monetary rewards for being tall is underway. The Bible doesn't make much of being tall. The people of Israel were warned that the people who resided in the Promised Land were taller than they. The only reference to a tall individual describes Saul as "from the shoulders upward higher than the people." Or head and shoulders above the crowd. Later the text reads: "Do not consider his appearance or his height because I have rejected him." That was God speaking.

The only reference to a short man in the Bible is to Zacchaeus, who had to climb a tree to see the parade because he was "little of stature." He fared better than Saul but I don't think one can, therefore, argue that God favors short persons either.

Saul's fate notwithstanding, I have always wanted to be taller, In our band of five brothers I was the shortest (least tall, I liked to say) and was always the last to be chosen when we played basketball. I know it is totally academic, but I even decided how tall I wanted to be—as tall as my brothers. But it didn't happen. Long ago I passed the age at which people get taller, and I have lived with the mostly subconscious notion that I would be happier if I had not been shorted. >>>

One morning, now some years ago, I looked in the mirror and the image that greeted me was of a short, fat, middle-age guy. I grumbled about the visage to Pat who said kindly, "You know there is one of those you can do something about." Actually there were two but I couldn't bring myself to lie about my age, so I went out and bought high-heeled boots which brought me up to standard and I have worn them ever since. My newest pair of Florsheims came in the mail today.

You ought to see me now. I am taller than most guys my height.

NOVEMBER 5

A New Word

Mendacious. I heard the word two times in a news commentary last evening. It's an uncommon word that journalists have begun to use to avoid calling politicians outright liars. I read the word often this season while perusing political punditry in news media.

Ever wonder how much of what one says may be inadvertently mendacious? I think if one is inclined to embellish the reports of one's achievements, one risks innocently stepping over the edge of truthfulness. (Of course, I don't ever do that.) But to stand before the national TV audience and boldly make statements that are untrue and then expect political support from the electorate seems to me to be intentionally mendacious as well as blatantly audacious. I have become weary of all the political drivel coming from persons who aspire to be the leader of a populace that deserves more. To have to choose the one who wanders less from the truth is insulting. I derive little hope from the thought that the electorate should be content with the littlest liar among the choices.

There I did it! I wanted to see if I was smart enough to register my impatience with all the prevarication perpetrated by politicians in their propaganda, while using all the words available to politely call all other candidates for the highest office liars. Remember that presidents-elect (and elected presidents for that matter) have the potential to demonstrate that anybody can be president or, alternatively, show that we don't really need a president. Choose carefully.

Oh, the mendacity of it all.

NOVEMBER 7

Helga Died Today

Three days short of her 100th birthday Helga's earthly sojourn is over. I was not startled by the news. I had been alerted to her recent move "to Lutherhaven where folks can look after me a bit more closely," she wrote. She had been caring for herself in her own place until she "tumbled," as she put it, and fell. Trauma from the accident hastened her demise, which unfortunately is often the outcome of missteps by the elderly.

In my last note to Helga I wrote:

> I hope you have recovered from your tumble and are moving about easily. I was going to tell you to be careful, but I think perhaps you have enough people telling you to be careful. On the other hand, I don't suppose anybody lives to be 100 years old by not being too careful. By the way, how did that happen—that is, living to be 100? Was it because of sturdy Danish genes, a lot of good luck, or was it because you were always a step ahead of trouble? I know that your 100th birthday is coming up soon. One hundred candle flames will certainly brighten that day. I wish I could be there to help you blow out the candles.
>
> I think it's quite remarkable that two people whose paths crossed eighty years ago had a chance to meet again. I was three years old when you left Minnesota for California in 1929. I am sure you remember much more about our first encounter than I. Take care, Helga. Stay healthy. You are the only hundred-year-old pen pal I have. 　　　>>>

Two years ago, from what seemed out of nowhere, Helga wrote a letter to tell me of a time when our lives touched briefly. She was a distant cousin of my mother who baby-sat my siblings and me eighty years ago, before baby-sitting had been invented. I met her briefly two summers ago. Helga was the last living person who held and cared for me when I was a babe. Her letter began a short, but delightful, correspondence. She was my only centenarian pen pal.

My pen pal is gone, but I have her letters.

NOVEMBER 10

Sermon on the Road

My files contain a collection of papers I am reluctant to discard. I could simply delete them, but they were created before I recorded my thoughts with my iMac. These are handwritten manuscripts of sermons I preached during my itinerancy as lay pastor at a small, rural church ninety miles away for nearly a decade, staying all the while with my day job at the college. Paging through what seem to be hastily scribbled notes persuaded me that the Sundays we worshiped with that small congregation were days that counted— mostly for me perhaps.

A lot of personal history resides in the texts of these homilies. They reveal my spin on the social, political, and intellectual ambiance of the time— the decade of the seventies. But it is the titles I assigned to these 20-minute talks that interest me in retrospect. Twenty minutes was all the time needed to exhaust my weekly store of wisdom and spiritual counsel. It was also about the time many of these busy ranchers quit listening. It was a good fit.

It is remarkable how readily the titles reveal thirty-some years later what was going on in my mind and happening in society at the time. With only a quick glance at each of these titles, I believe I could quite accurately reconstruct the text. Not infrequently when reminiscing about those days a parishioner will recall a title. It is possible that the titles may have been the most effective feature of these sermons. I have been recounting those days. Here's a list to ponder:

The Big Fight

The Dirty Dozen

Going Back to Where I Come From

The Great Masquerade

Biography of a Soul

The Portable Cross

Follow the Loser

The Empty Page

Foolish Barn Builder

Meanwhile, Back at the Ranch

Dumb Things I Gotta Do

The Three Stooges

Sermonus Innominatus

Then again, maybe you had to have been there.

NOVEMBER 11
Ain't Gonna Study War No More

Today is Veterans Day, one of our national holidays on which bankers, postal workers, and school children get to stay home and do whatever they choose. There may be a parade and there are always ceremonies at the gravesites of generations of war veterans. Before 1954, the annual commemoration of veterans was called Armistice Day. The practice was initiated to commemorate the signing of the Armistice on November 11, 1918, at the close of World War I. Literate persons know all this, I assume, but this is not about the holiday per se. It's about how we remember war.

My mother often told of being with a roomful of rural school children on that day in 1918 when nations decided enough war for now. Her teaching was interrupted by the arrival of the School Board come to dismiss the students and ring the school bell in celebration. She awaited the return of four brothers from the trenches in Europe. Armistice Day was a big deal in the early years of my boyhood.

Then there was World War II, my generation's war. Those warriors were included in the recognition, and the day became Veterans Day. Now we have veterans from the Korean War, Viet Nam War, Gulf War, and the current war in Iraq.

Inevitably, given the country's engagement in Iraq, our attention to war in recent weeks has been over the top; for example, public television's weeklong documentary on World War II. There have been numerous films about

World War II battles, notably the Normandy invasion. I was a rookie in basic training at that time.

It seems that our television screens are never far away from war movies these days. I have called a moratorium on watching war movies. I have viewed recent showings of these movies with troubling ambivalence. Generally, I have stood proudly at public recognition of veterans. I have even been heard telling grandchildren war stories. (Not being a hero, I am free to do that.) But I won't do that for a while until I unravel my uncertainty about whether I should stand amidst the vets or move to the sidelines. Being reminded too frequently by troubling images of dead and wounded soldiers, I contend with guilt when I accept the glory and honor that belongs to them. Not unlike the athlete who accepts the Super Bowl ring even though he spent all but one play on the bench. At best, I can only say, "I was there after the game was won." I intend to accept my recognition as warrior, if not reluctantly, at least with newfound modesty.

Quite likely the U.S. government will present my heirs with a neatly folded American flag at my demise. I secretly hope it will be a small one.

NOVEMBER 13

Seesaw Memories

A favorite old but unfamiliar saw goes like this: '*I see,*' *said the blind man, as he picked up his hammer and saw.* Apart from being punny, I like it because it speaks to my fondness for saws both literal and literary in a somewhat enigmatic way.

This brings me to the aim of this bit of recall about another of my favorite old saws. My old, radial arm saw has been standing idle in the garage for many months. It is (or was) a top-of-the-line Sears Craftsman model, which I acquired in 1967 to complete the first of many memorable carpentry capers spanning four decades. It had reached the end of its effective usefulness and reluctantly I had to attend to its final destiny.

Constrained by my commitment to sensible environmental responsibility, I could not unceremoniously toss it in the trash. I attempted to disassemble it for recycling. The tired old machine refused to go quietly. The bolts in its heavy frame were tight and rusted. They seemed to say, "Wait, let's think about this." And think about it I did.

I recalled the ease with which it sawed through heavy lumber, but remembered how lately it seemed to labor with heavy cuts when the circuit of its electric motor began to fail. Sound familiar? Carpentry, the love of which I learned from my father, became a healthy and delightful avocation, affording me pleasant distraction from the abstract world of professorial pursuits. With the faithful saw I built three houses, in addition to numerous smaller projects, such as fences, decks, and tree houses. There was the steep-roofed, forest chalet with a vaulted ceiling and expansive window wall to let in a magnificent view of the region's tallest mountain; a neighbor's modest house with a non-traditional mansard roof; and, of course, our legendary multifaceted dwelling with its central, spiral staircase and dodecagonal footprint. During those summers of healthy, physical, creative, and gratifying work, my mind seesawed about whether I wanted most to be a carpenter or a professor. In fact, I wrote a book about the struggle.

The bolts loosened and the parts of the old saw have been relegated to the appropriate metal recycling bins, hopefully to be reincarnated in another saw for another ambivalent professor seeking to maintain balance on the tight-rope between the ladder of meritocratic scramble and the ground in the world of real things.

NOVEMBER 15

Found Out

A letter arrived today from a Minnesota conservationist asking what I knew about ancient Black Oak Lake, a shallow lake drained before my time by pioneer farmers to farm the rich lakebed.

His letter prompted this memory:

The only evidence of the ancient lake when I was a boy was a strip of oak trees on the old shoreline. Our family farm included a small three-cornered fragment of "the woods," as we called our bit of that forest. Those oak trees offered summer shade for our black and white milk cows, firewood for our stoves, and sturdy oak posts for our fences. We picked springtime wild flowers and harvested gooseberries for pie and jelly there. Perhaps the only time we entered the woods for reasons other than play was to rouse the cows early on summer days and escort them to the barn for the morning milking.

Occasionally I made my way to the woods alone. It was a place of mystery where my boyhood imagination soared. I cherished the solitude—relief from the boisterous sibling hubbub. Free from reminders that excursions into the neighbor's woods were forbidden, I bravely strayed across the fence. With my imaginary spear fashioned from an oak splinter I stalked the neighbor's cows, which became a herd of black and white buffalo, carefully avoiding the bull whose reputation for irritability was neighborhood lore. My spear became a shotgun when I invaded the raven rookery and was made to defend myself against threatening angry adults. >>>

On one such solitary sortie into our neighbor's woods, I scaled a large oak to investigate a bundle of twigs near the top. As I neared the nest the branches bowed so steeply I was unable to maintain my grasp. My plunge was momentarily delayed by a dead branch, which not only eased my fall but also flipped me over. Badly scraped but otherwise unhurt, I landed on my back looking into the face of Mr. Norman, our mysterious neighbor and the landlord of the forbidden forest.

Prior to this sudden introduction, I had not met Mr. Norman, but I was familiar with the local legends encompassing him. He was the oldest man in our corner of the county, a Norwegian immigrant like my father. A successful farmer, he had the biggest barn and the largest herd of Holsteins with an enormous, black and white bull. A tall stern man about whom we had been cautioned never to trespass into the inviting black forest across the fence, it was unclear whether Mr. Norman or the massive Holstein bull was the greater danger.

Mr. Norman was the unfortunate victim of cancer, which at that time was a mysterious malady thought by some to be brought about by some secret trespass known only by the sufferer and God. He covered his face with a red bandanna to veil the dreadfully disfiguring surgical attempts to arrest the cancer. It was at his feet in his pasture, face up, in full view of his red-bandanna-shrouded face that I landed, momentarily breathless and totally uncertain about my future. I did the first thing that came to my battered eight-year-old brain. I scrambled to my feet and, without a word, I ran.

I made my way home slowly, uncertain about the outcome of my misadventure. My mother's first words were, "Mr. Norman called. He wanted to know if you were all right."

NOVEMBER 16

Life is So Retro

Currently in our society there is a collective tendency to make comparisons in fashion and design to styles from the past. When elements of style from the past appear in fashions, homes and automobiles, the result is said to be 'retro.' for instance, the recently redesigned Volkswagen beetle. It seems some elements of the past are worth repeating. It may also suggest a dearth of contemporary imaginative thinking. On the other hand, if essentials from the past enhance the present, it might indicate that the past wasn't devoid of good ideas, suggesting that there may have been something good about 'the good old days.'

I was mildly surprised to notice the profusion of words, which build on the prefix *retro*. One is retrospection, which emerges frequently in my counting days of life in the exit lane. Another of these retro words pertinent to understanding life in retrospect is retrofit, defined to modify by adding parts or devices not originally included.

Most oldsters are retrofitted to some extent, given the technological advances that have supplied us artificial joints, lens implants, arterial stents, cardiac valves, dentures, cochlear implants, etc. You get the picture.

I can hardly resist saying to my friend, who delights in cataloging his retrofixin's, "Oh Joe, you are so retro."

NOVEMBER 19

Who's Counting?

Not only does the Bible tell us that our days are numbered, it is also written: *As for you, even the hairs on your head have all been counted.* That's a bit surprising given all the other things God must have to do.

When I began college classes at the advanced age of twenty-seven my once very-black hair had begun to turn gray. I overheard a student identify me to another student as "the gray haired guy in our class." Being gray as a young adult and on through middlelescence was cool, as young people say. All of this is to say that by the time most people begin to have white hair, I had been there for years and it ceased to be cool.

People were often generous in their comments about my hair and my self-image came to rest on my full head of pewter colored hair and my Scandinavian surname. But time has taken its toll on that like it does on everything else. While I am a bit behind in the hair loss schedule, that number once known only to God is declining quickly. Because of that and the realization that folks simply can't or won't learn to spell or say my name correctly, my self-image has become badly bruised. I could count it all among the accumulated losses of aging; but while I can't do anything about the hair thing, I still insist loudly that my name is Stien (not Stein). I can't countenance not knowing who I am, a fearsome fate facing many oldsters. >>>

The account of numbered hairs appears among comments about the extent of God's love and knowledge about individuals. Agnostic friends say, "That's a crazy concept of God. What kind of God has time for that?"

All I will say is, I would not be much impressed with a God who doesn't.

NOVEMBER 22

A Two-part Story

A regular guest on Public Television's News Hour reads essays, which frequently inquire about the nature of contemporary American life in terms of individuals' sense of who they are. I am not convinced that Everyman thinks as much about that as he would have us believe. But I confess that my geriatric review of the pieces of life that shaped me is precisely that.

Recently, he argued that we humans live with a two-component self-image consisting of recollections of ourselves as children simultaneously with an awareness of our adult self-perceptions. I don't know how he would know that to be true other than as extrapolation based on his personal ruminations. He would further submit that whatever inner peace or disquiet we live with is the result of some kind of ongoing attempt to reconcile this lifelong cluster (perhaps clutter) of accumulated self-images and their attending attitudes. This may be profound or it may be obvious. I suspect it is the latter.

I am inclined to agree with the TV guy that we all are composed of a lifetime of self-images coarsely ground up into a kind of aggregate. And if one looks closely enough, some of the bigger chunks will be more evident than others.

With nostalgic recollections of Thanksgiving days decades ago pressing heavy on my mind, I am more aware today of the fragments than the synthesis. I will probably tell the youngsters at our table how (in my boyhood days) we selected our turkey or goose from our flocks, slaughtered and prepared it for roasting in what was an oven in a wood-burning stove skillfully regulated by my mother. There were no thermostats then, only my mother's intuitive sense of how much firewood was enough but not too much. I will likely remind them that, like the turkey, the firewood didn't come from the store. Nor did the potatoes in the bin in the cellar, nor the rye flour carefully ground and sifted by my parents. The apples and the pumpkin in the pies conjure images of harvests, not items on a grocery list. And, oh, yes—the pickles, pickled at home. The accumulation of pots and pans and the stacks of dishes didn't go in the dishwasher, but were washed by hand in water heated on the same wood-burning stove. You know the story. You have all heard it before.

But this is not about Thanksgiving per se with all of its festive creative culinary display and caloric overload. Nor is it necessarily about nostalgic recollections of bright spots in the synthesis of life.

Life may be more than the sum of its parts, but on some days the parts stand out.

NOVEMBER 24

Giving Thanks

In this counting of days, I have discovered that every day is the day before something. And every day is the day after something. True, but not necessarily profound. Today is the day before Thanksgiving Day—a day set apart by our society to recall all we have to be grateful about. That doesn't mean, does it, that we can't be grateful today, tomorrow, or the day after tomorrow?

Of course, I realize that Thanksgiving is intended to focus our collective gratitude. We are invited to participate without restraint with the rest of humankind, which can't be bad, can it? But to what extent does one's private gratitude depend upon a grateful society? Pejoratively perhaps, but I wonder if folks treat Thanksgiving Day as a once-a-year opportunity to get being grateful out of the way for another year.

During the years of my tenure as a preacher I learned that the most difficult sermons to prepare were those due at Thanksgiving time. While it might seem that gratitude is a simple concept, it is in my judgment one of our most complex emotions. I tried to sort it all out in a sermon I called Grace, Guilt and Gratitude. Gratitude is not an abstraction. There must be a source from which our good fortune comes.

Did you ever feel guilty about having so much when others have so little? That's probably not bad, if it restrains one from thinking that one is entitled to or has earned the good thing. If one buys a turkey to give to poor folks—whether motivated by guilt or motivated by gratitude—it's a good thing to do.

If it goes to someone who doesn't deserve good deeds or plump turkeys, it might be an act of grace. But who isn't worthy of good deeds? I can't believe God has poor people in this world so the rest of us will have reason to be generous or grateful. I believe God prefers us to be grateful for His deeds not ours.

I have become content to let God sort it out.

NOVEMBER 25

Desperate Disparity

Extended families gather more frequently during this season of Thanksgiving, Christmas, and New Year's Day than any other comparable period of weeks. It is not uncommon in these days of easy travel and extended longevity for these gatherings to include four generations. That will be the scene at our house this Thanksgiving Day when our children, their children, and their children's children gather at our house.

But this is not about Thanksgiving per se with all of its festive, creative, culinary display and caloric overload. It's about an opportunity to observe expressions of gratitude. Pat efficiently manages the festivities with the capable assistance of our daughters and granddaughters. Except for maintaining the fire in the fireplace, there is little for me to do other than observe.

We feast in plenty, in comfort in the warmth of the fireplace, and in the embrace of those God gave us especially to love. We solicit from each other, in turn, what it is that we are most grateful for. Then we retire, each to his or her preferred individual gadget or entertainment, while we wait for Gramom's pumpkin pie—relaxed and grateful.

I consider distracting their attention from the football game, the video games, cell phones, iPods, and even some good books to ask them to wonder what it might be like to have absolutely nothing about which to be thankful—unimaginable in our land of bounty. Visions of circumstances so disparate from our own in which people live in despair and desperate need of everything would only add to the discomfort from having eaten too much, I suppose.

Irony at its best—or worst.

NOVEMBER 26

Signs

Not unlike a lot of towns, our city has a street named Howard. Occasionally, as we pass by Howard Street folks say, "There's your street." I confess that I have wondered after whom the street was named. I know it wasn't I. And heaven forbid that I was named after a street. As to whether crossing or driving on Howard Street messes with my mental rumination anymore than driving, say, on Lincoln Street, I adamantly say "No way."

That is, until today. While on an errand today I drove by a familiar intersection of Howard and Regal, a neighborhood junction I have traversed countless times. What startled me today was not the Howard Street sign, which simply contained the word HOWARD, but directly below were the bold words DEAD END. While I don't think I am obsessed with thoughts about mortality, I admit to wondering if one should be watching for advance warning signs (especially oldsters driving the EXIT ONLY lane).

For some time I have been intrigued with a couple of highway signs marking the turn-off to Dinosaur National Monument in South Dakota. Accompanying those notices are signs, which read: DINOSAUR DEAD AHEAD and ROAD TO EXTINCTION.

Why encountering Howard Dead End should conjure images of those South Dakota words of warning was troubling,

I haven't decided. But tonight after dark I will remove the neighborhood sign, just to make sure.

The disquiet is actually quite noisy.

NOVEMBER 27

Going Home

My well-worn Funk & Wagnalls Standard College Dictionary allows more space to defining and explaining the word *home* than most of its many other words. Yet I have three dictionaries of synonyms that list no substitutes for the word, which may only attest to the limitation of those three volumes. Oddly, neither do they show a synonym for *synonym*.

One would think that the idea of home would be simply understood as the place where one lives. But then, what does one do with the notion that a person might be living away from home or being at home away from home? Anyone who has given any thought at all to home knows that this simple word is fraught with subtle innuendoes—a place, a feeling, a house, a metaphor.

Biologists write about homing instinct, a tendency and ability of animals to make their way back to a place of significance in their past. Few humans accept the notion that much of human behavior, if any, is instinctive. I wouldn't argue loudly that the tendency is innate, but I tend to believe that most of us harbor feelings of varying intensity about some place which is or was home to us. Probably the most intense experience of the yearning for home is homesickness in children.

In our modern, transient society many, if not most of us, have moved frequently and probably think of the place where we presently live as home more than some other place—distant both in time and space which beckons us to return. The song, *Home for the Holidays*, conjures idyllic images of fireplace warmth, snowy scenery, festive meals quite likely embellished by time—a place preserved in memories stored in one's heart, mind, soul, or wherever such nostalgia lingers.

For me home is not an abstraction. It's a real place in western rural Minnesota, although admittedly somewhat impressionistic. It is now mostly space, devoid of the physical features that loom large in mind--the house, barn, well, gravel pit, oak grove, pasture—once real spaces in which we lived and moved about in real time now long past. Still I return to stand where it all was and let the wistfulness wash over me.

It's home, a place, a feeling, a house, a metaphor.

NOVEMBER 28

Light

Beginning the day after Thanksgiving Day folks have begun hanging lights on their houses, fences, and shrubbery—even their dogs. Each year the number of light bulbs seems to increase exponentially. It is the season of light.

It's been 2,000 years since what many believers call The First Christmas. My first Christmas was in 1926. (You do the math.) I don't remember anything about it. However, two scenarios stand out in my recollections of some of my early holiday experiences. Our Christmas trees were lighted with candles clipped to the branches. I recently saw some of those quaint metal clips at an antique display, which I assume caused this retreat into memory. Not only did the dozens of small candle flames brighten the corner of the living room of the otherwise dimly lit farmhouse or the dais of the old country church, it sparked the imagination and hope of one, small, reticent farmboy—images of good things now and hope for things to come. Christmas still has that enchantment, but it is not engendered by trees or houses lighted by electricity. There is more to it.

The other vivid image of Christmas past is the festive table replete with all of the tasty dishes the bounty of our farm, garden, heritage, and culinary skill of my Danish mother could muster. The lutefisk came from our Norwegian father's homeland. Nothing eclipses the anticipation of hungry, growing farm boys. But that's a story for another time. There is no mention of decorations or banquets in the original Christmas story. It is all about light—blazing skies and brilliant stars—and the response of people to this Light come into the world, which in truth is what Christmas is all about.

Elegantly lighted exteriors fade in the brilliance of the real Star.

NOVEMBER 30

Impatient Patients

While splitting firewood, the wedge I was holding took an untoward bounce and the sledge struck my hand resulting in an ugly gash on my index finger. It wasn't particularly painful and I continued my task. Later Pat won the debate about whether the injury required attention and we made our way to the emergency room seeking a second opinion. We signed in and patiently perused the disarray of reading material presented to impatient patients as something to do while counting the minutes they have already waited.

I have had occasion throughout these overtime years to linger (or languish) in the reception rooms of several different doctors. One can get a feel for the interests of the medical group as well as their assessment of the sophistication of their patrons by perusing the reading material they provide for those who wait. Sports Illustrated is more at home in physical therapy or chiropractic holding-pens than Fortune Magazine or Golfing, more often read (or reread) in the offices of specialists like dermatologists. I am not sure I could suggest appropriate reading for octogenarians marking time in a doctor's office. It is probably not Fortune Magazine and long-term investments. But I digress. This is not about outdated magazines. It is about ER protocol.

Eventually I was escorted to an examination room and left to wait some more. Thinking about my pile of yet to be split firewood my anxiety and impatience rose steadily. An orderly strolled in and began to make casual conversation. His ID badge identified him as Patient Advocate, which given the present circumstances amused me no little bit. Uncertain about his role, I inquired whether the word patient on his ID was a noun or an adjective. Was he advocating for patients or promoting patience, I wondered.

Patient patients fare well in the ER.

December

DECEMBER 1

Grandfather by Proxy

Counseling undergraduate students about their academic aspirations, progress, or schedules was an indispensable aspect of my professorial tasks. Occasionally it was necessary that a student be told to "get off the dime and get to work" or that the grade he had been assigned was fair, if not generous. But rarely were these conversations unpleasant. Careful not to make psychological assessments, I talked with them (listened mostly) about their personal, emotional disquiet. One sunny spring afternoon three well-adjusted, competent students, coping with news that their parents were considering divorce, came by seeking assurance that they were not to blame. Usually, however, and to my delight the young folks dropped in to engage in some conversation or debate about intellectual matters. That was teaching at its best and always a welcome diversion from grading papers, writing memos, and completing committee reports.

One day a popular, happy, successful student stopped by. After thirty minutes of casual chatter about the way things were, she said abruptly, "Well, I gotta go now." Uncertain about why she had come, I asked if there was something specific she wished to talk about. "Not really," she said, "I miss my Dad and you are a lot like him. I just wanted to chat."

A decade or two later a similar scenario emerged. Only this time the young woman (a different one) said that she missed her grandfather and I reminded her of him, so she came by to visit.

Nothing had changed except I had grown older.

DECEMBER 5

Obitus

For reasons I am reluctant to examine closely I have begun to glance a bit less casually at the obituary announcements in our newspaper. There may be a time after which reading these notices becomes compulsory. I have noticed that I have reached an age which exceeds the average of those whose obituaries appeared today. If one needs to know if one is on schedule, it may be well to check the numbers regularly. Whether I may have reached that time is not what this piece is about. It's about the phenomenon; that is, the practice of publishing these postmortem bios.

I may have to write A Guide for Necrologists. There seem to be no rules giving direction to this genre. Whether they serve the quick or the dead is unclear. Today I read the obituary of an acquaintance. It was a typical one-size-fits-all kind of piece. Beyond informing me of his demise, it didn't serve my friend well. Of course, he had parents, a wife and children, and a vocation or profession—most everybody does. His identity was not in question. The piece didn't catalogue the many reasons for which we should cherish his memory.

While I am convinced that one should live one's life so that those writing obituaries or speaking eulogies won't have to tell lies, I am ambivalent about whether it matters much to the departed. Just to be safe, however, I am contemplating writing my own obituary.

It will appear under the title FINIS at the end of this run.

DECEMBER 6

To Do or Not To Do

A question often asked by folks contemplating retirement is how one can know when the time is right. The only advice I have to offer is that, if you need to know before you can sleep what you will do the next day, you should not retire. To agonize about whether one is gainfully retired is to compromise the perquisites of post-professional life. Retirement was meant to provide time for some freedom not to do some things.

Days of retirement, however, are no more devoid of decisions than are days in other phases of life. One might argue that neonates face very few, if any, choices. That circumstance wanes quickly and infants soon learn to voice their preferences and not always quietly. It might be said that life is essentially a sequence of decisions—to do or not to do. It may also be said that life is the consequence of one's choices.

None of this, however, absolves one of the obligations intrinsic in living peacefully with others. There are always lists of things one ought to do. One of the brighter aspects of this time of stepping aside to watch the rest of society constrained by the rules of work is the liberty to loaf and linger leisurely with the morning paper and a second cup of coffee contemplating the freedom to do or not to do. My motto regarding challenges had always been: "If it can be done, I can do it." My refrain has become: "If it can be done, I can do it if I want to."

I don't always want to.

DECEMBER 7

The Record

During a recent stay at the hospital, confusion about whether I was there was confounded by some persistent uncertainty about who I am—or maybe who I was. There had been no little confusion about my identity since I arrived. My family name, STIEN, is a bit unusual and folks seem reluctant to let it be that way. It seems they would rather it be STEIN. What many have come to think unusual is my insistence that others (all others) spell it the same way I do—with the I before the E.

During my brief stay it was amazing to watch the accumulation of a vast stack of papers kept in a folder in my room. Nobody suggested that I read it nor did anyone say that I should not. It did occur to me that it might be interesting reading and that it just might contain some information that would help me tell folks who I am, which seemed to be of interest to everyone who came into the room—especially those dispensing medicine.

So I read the document regularly (when no one was watching). I didn't understand much of it, inasmuch as it was written mostly in acronyms. What I did discover, however, was that on every other page the name of some chap named Stein appeared, and I began to understand why people attending to my needs invariably asked, "Are you Mr. Stien or are you Mr. Stein?" I began to wonder whose pills I was taking. >>>

Some of the more alert attendants looked at my wristband to ascertain my identity, which was OK with me. After I noticed that the spelling of my name had suffered the usual careless abuse (or that my identity was uncertain), the first band they gave me was discarded. Fortunately, I was not too ill to enjoy observing the hospital's attempts to discover not only what was ailing me but also to establish who I was.

I am not certain I was able to convince the record keeper who I am. I left physically intact, but with my identity battered a bit by this escapade. I also left concerned about that guy, Stein, whose identity was so carelessly discarded when his wristband was removed from my wrist and unceremoniously tossed into the wastebasket.

I wonder where he went.

DECEMBER 8

Praise or Worship

Oh, for a thousand tongues to sing our Great Redeemer's praise is the first line in one of my favorite hymns. Charles Wesley wrote the words in 1739; the music and the text have survived since then. They have great staying power. Our congregation doesn't sing this great old hymn much anymore, and when we do the words are sung to incongruous, jazzed-up rhythms accompanied by guitars and drums. Obviously, this offends my sense of propriety about the worship of a majestic God. I can't conceive of God as a happy-hour buddy.

I have considered the possibility that my elderly fellow worshippers and I have passed the time in our lives when we have become unable to let go of fixed preferences—incapable or unwilling to embrace change. After all, I spent my professional life encouraging young people to consider change. I am also nagged by the thought that God may not be the guardian of propriety and frowns on my critique of the worship style of other believers. But I still cherish the grand old hymns.

So what is an oldster like me to do? I can stand by sullenly quiet while the youngsters clap, bounce and sway, and loudly sing redundant songs devoid of musical or textual sophistication. Or I can wait for my turn to sing lustily, but solemnly, the token grand, old, majestic hymn with pipe organ accompaniment and let God judge the relative merit or virtue of songs of praise vs. hymns of worship.

DECEMBER 11

A Christmas Pageant

I have now lived long enough to wonder if Christmas ever loses its luster for folks who are traveling the exit lane. The activities and conversations in the glow of the Christmas tree are invariably centered on younger themes. I am in no way feeling neglected or overlooked. Our lives have been stuffed with all the good fortune and good will that Christmas in its entire splendor has to offer.

Yet I have never seen a Christmas pageant, crèche or front yard diorama that included a couple of old guys who had minor roles in the Christmas drama. The ancient story is bracketed fore and aft by accounts of two retirees who were only peripherally involved in the main stage events.

Zacharias, the father of John the Baptist, was struck dumb because he didn't believe the prologue to the story. But he could still see—and seeing is believing. He lived to see promise fulfilled. Simeon, an old man hanging around the temple, held the Infant Jesus and said: *Now let your servant depart in peace, Lord, according to your word. For I have seen with my own eyes your salvation, which you have prepared before the face of all peoples.*

I think we stop reading the account of Christmas before we hear the whole story. Perhaps I should write a pageant that moves these old-timers away from the edges and into the mainstream of the story.

I'm thinking I could be one of the old dudes in my pageant.

from Christmas Letters, 2007

DECEMBER 12

A Moose or Two

Wildlife has always fascinated me. My parents encouraged us to observe and respect the wild critters we encountered on our farm. There were cottontail rabbits, squirrels, skunks, badgers, raccoons, weasels, despicable rats, and an occasional fox in our fields, meadows, and woodlot. There were the game birds—ducks, geese, and pheasants—and, of course, the ubiquitous and numerous songbirds. Parental decree sheltered the songbirds from our slingshots.

On Pat's North Dakota family farm where we spent our early years trying to be farmers we regularly encountered all of those creatures plus coyotes, white tail deer, and scores of jackrabbits.

Since our university student and professorial days we have lived in urban or suburban settings. Our current house at the edge of town sits at the foot of a north-slope strip of pine and fir trees on steep, rocky land not suited for houses. Wisely we faced the large living room windows toward this forest. We have grown accustomed to watching deer, coyotes, raccoon, countless quail, turkeys, and an occasional porcupine stroll casually within feet of the windows. A resident doe and her yearly twin fawns are regulars in our hillside scenario. We are at home with this urban wildlife, as my ecology professor colleague calls them—creatures who were here long before we came and have somehow adjusted to our being here. >>>

Being a biologist I could discourse at length and eloquently, I believe, about these critters, fascinating variations on one of Nature's favorite themes. And speaking of variants, one of the strangest appeared in our window this morning. Returning from retrieving the morning paper, I was startled by a huge moose munching on snowberries 20 feet from our front door. She glanced at me and, essentially ignoring me, continued browsing. Five minutes later she moved into full view of our living room couch, bedded down twenty feet from the house and began to doze. Soon from nowhere her half-grown calf joined her.

Believe me, nothing livens a city dweller's morning coffee more than a cud-chewing moose or two peering into the living room window!

DECEMBER 13

Entropy

Early in my education in scientific thought I learned of the tendency of complex, natural systems to go bananas. The phenomenon is called entropy—the idea that an ordered system lacking energy input will naturally move towards disorder. An analogy that I frequently employed attempting to help students comprehend entropy was to describe the ubiquitous disarray of their dormitory rooms and to suggest that without the expenditure of some energy an orderly dorm space will naturally move to a disordered space. The analogy failed mostly because few students understood the concept of an orderly dorm room.

Students' incomprehension not withstanding, entropy is real and nothing calls attention to the tendency more clearly than the bumps we encounter along the road to physical well-being. Life is not exempt from entropy. Wellness is essentially staying ahead of the disordering forces—germs, accidents, worn out parts, toxins, etc.

It seems that as the years accumulate, the bumps in the road are more difficult to avoid. A sign reading Bumpy Road Ahead might be appropriate for folks far down the road. We were reminded today (we had to call 911) that there is no 'go home free' card in the game of being. We knew that, but we have been allowing ourselves to believe the "Wow, you look great" flattery to distract us from the realities of our biosity.

Pat is OK and we are both grateful for a bit of reprieve.

DECEMBER 16

Christmas Letters

All of our out-going Christmas letters are in the mail and there are still nine days until Christmas, which leaves me time to ponder this practice and my participation in it. I can't recall the first time I read a Christmas greeting, much less the first time I sent one. It is a custom into which one is born, I suppose, or eventually adopts for reasons that are as varied as folks who do it.

Christmas cards have always been, more or less, part of our family's holiday tradition. Pat and I have been getting and begetting Christmas letters for the better part of sixty years. I would like to believe my involvement is sustained by my soul's annual infusion of the spirit by the angelic proclamation of good tidings of great joy.

While it is good to be remembered, one suspects (judging from the perfunctory nature of some of the cards we receive) that the practice too easily becomes dutiful, devoid of any sentiment about the grandeur of the event we are observing. All of which causes me to wonder about what truly moves me to write a one-page-fits-all Christmas letter. Surely my motivation is more virtuous than to display the deftness of my letter writing skills.

I am unsure.

DECEMBER 19

Speechless in Seattle

We are saddened today by the news from a very special friend in Seattle. His wife of sixty-five years and a talented musician is experiencing the devastation of Alzheimer's disease. He wrote of the sadness of watching Ruth, who at one time could remember countless scores of music, unable to remember what a piano was for. She moves farther and farther from everything and everybody, he said. He wrote of the challenge, at age 85, of caring for her 24 hours a day.

Loren was a pastor, our pastor, decades ago. He offered wise counsel, which served me well in the early days of my sojourn as a believer in transition from the actual fields of North Dakota to the esoteric terrain of ideas. In this recent letter he spoke of the dissonance between what he is experiencing and his years of being there for scores of people facing circumstances that seemed irreconcilable with a merciful God. "Now I don't know what to say," he wrote. "You be the minister. What should I say?"

I, too, am speechless. What does one say to a friend facing such a dreadful physical and spiritual challenge. This is what I wrote: "I, like you, ponder the seemingly irreconcilable conflicts of Scripture and life experiences. I can't help you with that, but can offer whatever comfort there may be in assuring you that we, too, are heavy hearted by what has happened and will continue to pray (in the face of all dissonance) for your health and that Holy God will hasten Ruth's release."

To whom else can we go?

DECEMBER 21

Public Education

To make a statement to a large and varied audience, bumper stickers are probably one's least expensive option. A personalized license plate is another, although it requires some skill to present a clear announcement within the limited space offered by most license plates. Words without vowels are vulnerable to misinterpretation. Then there is also the matter of vanity. Why should anyone reading license plates care what your name is? I do because my father, proud of his Norwegian heritage, taught me to care.

A former student called yesterday requesting a letter of recommendation—one of the more pleasurable remnants of life in the academy. While I was pleased to write the letter, I admit being a little annoyed that she had misspelled my name and entered it incorrectly into the record. I signed my letter STIEN as I invariably do because that is the correct spelling. Consequently, it will appear in Cheryl's folder two ways. My experience, however, is that no one will recognize the error or wonder who is right.

Having my name misspelled so often has moved me to educate the public about the proper spelling of my name. I pay fifty dollars in addition to the base fee for a personalized license plate, which displays my message I-B4-E for the driving public to see. The effectiveness of the endeavor is unclear. Most folks who comment about it assume that I am or was an English teacher, a notion that (even if true) I would hardly confess publicly. A few bright persons guess the message has something to do with our name, but it's slow going.

Can you imagine old Albert not being annoyed by IENSTIEN?

DECEMBER 22

Expectations

The story is told of a mother without food for her hungry children. She had no fuel for the oven and nothing to bake. She took two stones, placed them in the cold oven, and prayed that God would turn the stones into bread. After some time she opened the oven and found the stones unchanged to which she replied, "I didn't think it would work." Prayer from that premise may be tantamount to buying a lotto ticket with the expectation that it won't be a winner. But this is not about the probability of either answered prayer or winning the lottery. It is about life and expectation.

Life is an exercise in expectation. We expect the sun to rise, snow to be cold, fire to burn, and water to quench thirst. We don't expect everyone to love us, nor to be happy every day. But life cannot be lived without expectation, nor will it end without expectation.

One learns what to expect and what not to expect. It's the distinction that gives one direction. However, I have noticed lately that getting older limits one's expectations. One doesn't expect to live forever. Nor does one expect romance, adventure, the pursuit of fame or fortune to provide the primary motivational energy for one's latter-day thoughts and activities. Few octogenarians aspire for reputation or wealth beyond that already attained. Expecting high-sustained levels of health may be naïve. Whatever pinnacle one looks down from is quite different from views on the road to the top, and significantly different from that on the road leveling out.

Quite likely if you have read thus far you are thinking, "So?"

Frequently, when Pat and I visited aging Aunt Marcie in the care center where she lived her final weeks, we would encounter Mabel roaming the halls in her wheelchair calling for Ralph, who also moved about in a wheelchair (quietly though). When she found him she wailed in dementia, "What's going to happen to us? What's next?" His answer was always the same and to the point, "We die."

There are, in this life, things we can count on.

DECEMBER 25

Thoughts on Christmas Day

My thoughts bring me to the realization that Christmas is incomprehensible. It is meant to be believed, not understood. The three wise guys had been thinking about the one who was to be born King of the Jews and they went searching. They got lost, being wise men they asked for directions, found the child, and worshiped him (with contemporary or traditional music, we don't know). Now that I think about it, there were no traditions about how to worship God made flesh and dwelling among us. This was a new thing. They left gifts and went home the back way, and we hear no more about them. So much for the wise guys.

Then there were shepherds doing what shepherds do—watching their sheep. Clearly, they were unaccustomed to voices from the sky. Voices from the sky will scare anyone. Unlike the wise guys they weren't expecting anything, but one doesn't ignore voices in the sky, so they went. They had good directions. They found the stable and hung around and had their photo taken. (We have all seen the picture.) Before they went back to work they told a bunch of people what they had heard and seen. The Book with the story says no more about those sheepherders either, except that after they returned (to the sheep) they praised God. And they did it in the field—contemporary worship at it's finest.

When I was a boy I always wanted to be a wise guy in the Christmas pageant. They had the best songs to sing. But the teacher, bent on type casting, always had me be a shepherd. >>>

My brother Harold got to be an angel once. More type casting—after all, there were herald angels. Recently I have been nagged by the thought that all along I have been a shepherd wearing wise guy robes wanting to understand what God asks me to believe.

Now I wonder what's wrong with being a shepherd.

from Christmas Letters, 2000

DECEMBER 26

Presumption

My flight to Minneapolis departed early (6:30 AM). Because of some confusion among the security people, I boarded the airplane seconds before they closed the door. Consequently, my carry-on bag containing my enroute reading was stashed out of reach. Left with the ubiquitous airline periodical and the unchanging sea of clouds in the window, I soon became bored.

The pretty young woman in the next seat had been reading, with apparent delight, a magazine reporting the romantic escapades of film stars and other celebrities. Having finished the magazine and noticing my restless idleness she asked whether I wished to read it. To my "No thank you," she said politely, "I didn't think you would." Then she pulled from her satchel and offered me a copy of Smithsonian.

As I read about ancient pyramids, I allowed myself to be flattered by the notion that she recognized me as an urbane person with astute interests broader than the romantic trysts of public persons. I wondered what might have been her first clue. My comely white hair, my quiet pensive scholarly demeanor, my sartorially proper dress? It couldn't have been the latter. I was wearing boots, jeans and my favorite denim jacket, my preferred western get-up.

I read on about stem cell research and she was into the next issue of Hollywood Romance.

Then I realized, she had already read Smithsonian.

DECEMBER 27

Missing Words

A little girl in a group asked by Art Linkletter to draw pictures of what they wanted to be when they became adults was frustrated. "I want to be married when I get big," she said, "but I don't know how to draw that."

Except for an incorrigibly introspective few, most ordinary folks don't fuss much about what this experience called 'life' is all about—too busy breathing, I suppose. That's good, I argue, in that it allows one to get on with life and get some work done, even if that work is only musing. But life is mysterious and intangible, and my curiosity about it persists.

As the years pass, one's mind becomes crammed with trivia that has little to do with everyday well-being. There is a crevice in my brain stuffed with minutiae useful only in the trafficking of ideas about embryology. I learned a dictionary of jargon—triploblastic, epimorphic, ovoviviparous, histogenesis—words that come to mind more quickly than the name of a friend encountered unexpectedly. Except to speak with a practicing professional, I have no use for that lingo. I wonder why those words persist when the names of favorite folks become elusive.

I search my mind (or is it brain) for words that might give meaning to the notion of meaning. That lexicon is elusive. I don't find it among my professionally acquired vocabulary or in my everyday thesaurus. The jargon of philosophers helps little. While skeptics argue that we humans impute meaning where none exists, I haven't abandoned the belief that my life, in the great scheme of everything, must mean something. Can it be there are things we understand without words—things we can't draw?

I have heard it said that the one best able to say what life was all about was one who had just died.

If that's the case, I can wait.

DECEMBER 29

Goodbye, Good Brother

Today was unlike any other of all my accumulation of days. I left the bedside of Ray, my youngest brother and the last survivor of my four brothers, fully aware that I had had my last conversation with him. These were my thoughts during the long ride back to Minneapolis from whence I would later leave for home.

The course of events during the last hours of life is as unique as the person whose final moments have come. I had traveled to his bedside because he had asked me to come. I wondered what he would say to me, but equally about what I would say to him.

Although having been alerted to his pending passage, I found him alert and, though struggling for breath, anxious to talk, consciously aware of his imminent death. We talked (he more than I) about his confidence that God had not abandoned him. He was troubled that he had made promises to God that he had not kept. I assured him as best I could that God's grace covers even our broken promises.

He and I belonged to a band of five brothers. Struggling for breath, he reminisced about each of us and our congenitally imperfect youngest sister for whom he had a special fondness. Then, looking into my eyes, he said, "You were my idol. I love you." I believe he wanted me to know that and it was why he asked me to come. He uttered some other sentences but he had tired and spoke softly. Unfortunately, I didn't hear his last words to me. I am unable to give myself permission to wonder what he said.

Ray was the first and, for the most part, my only brother who could say to me without embarrassment, "I love you."

"Goodbye, good brother. I love you. Rest in peace," I said.

And he slept.

January

JANUARY 4

Having Fun Yet?

When it happens that some celebrity has been diagnosed with a serious health challenge, as has been the case recently, the media presumes to educate the public about the verities of the illness. We learn (again) about the survival rates, therapies, consequences and prognosis of the malady. These media scenarios are aired most frequently when cancer, given its many manifestations, is the offending challenge. I suppose all of this is in society's best interest, if the intent is to promote wise living and prevention.

I am suspicious that our interest is aroused most by the private and personal response of the victim to the life and death consequences of his or her illness. To know not only when one is going to die but also what will be the cause must certainly be an emotional challenge. I am not sure how much watching others, famous or not, meet the challenge is helpful—largely, I suspect, because it is not an instinctive tendency to project oneself into such a scenario.

It must, however, cross the mind of even the healthiest eighty-something oldsters (as well as those watching them) that they are going to die and quite likely sooner than later. And in many cases they will very likely know why.

I can't believe God puts ill or old persons in our midst so that we might learn how to manage end-of-life scenarios. But I do believe that unawareness or indifference to the those sequestered in Havens for the Aged may cause us to miss learning about the indignity of being regarded as spent personalities, destined to the scrap pile of human life. That's a fate worse than the final demise, whatever its cause.

I don't think Art Buchwald got it right. Dying isn't always fun.

JANUARY 5

Living in the Round

One could quite safely argue that in contemporary society there are few older people who have lived all of their lives continuously in one house. My experience I believe is typical. I have lived in fourteen different houses, excluding a few short stays in apartments. While it is interesting, I attach little significance to the observation that of those fourteen places my tenancy was longest in the very first and the last of these dwellings—our current home. What brings this reverie about houses in which I spent significant time I am unsure. I believe that in these later years of wandering thoughts, musing about stopovers along the way is good for one's perception of the journey. I do wonder (a perk of leisure) about how much, if anything, this parade of houses had to do with shaping the 'me' that I now am. I can easily recall significant events that occurred during most of these tenancies, but haven't yet unraveled the extent to which the houses were more than an indifferent set of props staging the drama. But now we live in a round house.

Completing unfinished areas in two of these houses and designing and actually building two others was a delightful diversion from the routine of professor work. A sentence in the back-cover notes on one of my books reads: *Dr Stien and his wife live in a twelve-sided, essentially round house the professor built one summer to clear his mind.* It is the latest in this series of houses about which I have been musing and is, without debate, the most interesting. It is also the one which has generated more innuendo about the quirks of the professorial mind. Colleagues practiced in circular logic are quick to notice the lack of corners in which to be trapped; the orbital hallway which always brings one back to where one started— a common academic experience; the spiral stairway as the optimal design for the rotation of deans.

When questioned about what moved us to build our house in the round, it had never occurred to me that it might have been inspired by all the palaver about academic circles. I just wanted to do something contrary, an ambition that circumscribes the thinking of most professors with time on their hands.

We have been living courageously in the round ever since.

JANUARY 9

Do Not Bend

It is surprising how past experiences totally unrelated to present tasks intrude into one's consciousness. This morning, as I was struggling to put on my socks, it seemed to me that my feet are moving beyond reach. My legs like those of many oldsters resist bending. While contending with this age-imposed stiffness, the memory of a decades-old scenario surfaced.

Early in my professional career I was sitting in an interview with the dean of a California community college where I had applied for a teaching position. Reading from a sheaf of papers early in our conversation, he said, "It says here that you are an unbending person. What do you think about that?"

Startled a bit I replied, "What I think about it depends on who said it." He suddenly seemed apologetic and said that ethically he couldn't reveal who said it. It was the only question he asked and went on to nattering about the college, its expectations and some details about the position, which seemed excessively structured, All the while I, a person of conviction, silently speculated about what may have motivated anyone to write that I was rigid, unyielding, and inflexible. When he finished and without soliciting other questions from me, he announced that the position was mine. (It was a period when science teachers were scarce.) Bewildered, I declined the invitation on the grounds that

I would not be comfortable in circumstances that precluded independent thinking.

I went on to a nearly four-decade sojourn in the professoriate where successful defense of intellectual high ground requires standing one's ground, and one's foothold in the meritocracy is what it's all about. Whether I overcame my predisposition not to bend is still uncertain.

But not so in my early morning tussle with my socks.

JANUARY 10
Triumph of Triviality

My resolve to write a brief review of my thoughts or activities of each day of my 81st trip around the sun turns out to be more ambitious than I had imagined. On some days there seems little to write about. Inasmuch as I am quite convinced that, as life is allotted to us in daily increments, each day is a gift. I am not yet resigned to the thought that some days may be trivial. Life may be likened to a house of cards in which no single card is trivial and the removal of any one of them dooms the structure. The analogy to days deemed nonessential is obvious.

No one would seriously deny that some days, in fact many of our days, are so lightly etched in our minds that memories of them seem not to exist. I have no recollection nor can I conjure any of the many other 10th days of January in my accumulation of days. What I can be certain about is that the counting didn't stop on any of them. With a little retrospection I can easily establish where I may have been on some of the 10th of January days:

1936   Minnesota blizzard

1943   High school days in cold Minnesota

1945   On the way to military duty in Europe

1948   Teaching rural elementary school children in North Dakota

1951   My first college semester   >>>

1958   My first university teaching assignment

1991   London with Pat and her theatre students

Other years January 10th seems to have passed unnoticed. It seems that significance is not allotted in daily increments. Life is more than the sum of all of our days, trivial or otherwise.

I am beginning to feel good about today!

JANUARY 11

Insignificance

An e-mail I received today from Dave, a former student now a successful physician/scientist, closed with the following sentence: "I hope that your contemplation of our insignificance proceeds apace and that this e-mail finds you well." I assumed that he was referring to something I had said either in letter or conversation.

It had been several years since I had heard from him. I last talked to him when he was a first-year medical student. He completed medical school and went on to earn a PhD in biochemistry and genetics, achievements of no little significance, I would say.

Indeed, I was pleasantly surprised to hear from Dave and learn of his professional success. I am proud and glad for him. However, I have outgrown my fantasy (naïve in retrospect) that I have had something to do with the success of my students. I am now content to have been a proud bystander absolved of the notion that significance accrued to me because I had been their professor. But I ponder Dave's reference to insignificance.

Three decades ago Pat and I lived in a house we built in the midst of a second-growth pine and fir tree forest. There were among these trees numerous large stumps, remnants of earlier logging operations. A pleasant pastime of mine in those years was to stroll among the trees, linger on one those stumps and ponder my insignificance. Tall trees will do that to one.

>>>

It was then I began to wonder if there might be more to insignificance than status in the meritocracy of academia. Dave was one of my students in those days. I wonder if I may have alerted him to the consolation of insignificance.

Yes, Dave, contemplation of my insignificance proceeds apace!

JANUARY 12
Hats Off

As well as I can recall, my fascination with head gear (especially hats) began with the black, wide-brimmed Stetson hat my grandfather wore when he prettied up to do business in town or go to church. When he died and his earthly treasure was divided among us, the black Stetson passed on to me. It was my sole material inheritance from him. How it came to me I don't know, but that's another story.

I wore Granddad's Stetson, profanely perhaps, in the fields making hay or harvesting as a teenage farmhand. Modesty constrains me from commenting about how I thought the hat bolstered my self-image. Time has obscured the ultimate destiny of the dusty old hat. Grandson Zachary has been seen occasionally wearing one of my collection of mostly retired headgear, but until now no one has staked a claim to any of them.

A display of one's hats and caps may serve well as a wordless biography or, better yet, as an obituary. Mine would include my seldom worn western hat (not the same as a cowboy hat), which I acquired at the 1974 Denver International Livestock Show. My host, a rancher friend, gave me the hat. He wanted me to look like a cattleman. It worked. A book peddler at the airport approached me with the wager, "I bet you're here for the cattle show."

"What gave me away?" I asked. >>>

There is the white hard-hat that kept my head clear on numerous construction sites. I wore it mostly when inspectors appeared and as a display of machismo for admiring females visiting the job site. Still in my collection are a couple of felt dress hats from post-war fashions later pronounced nonessential for a presidential image by JFK. One of my favorite hat styles is an Irish wool tweed I acquired in Oxford, England. I did more for that hat than it did for me. It was the one Zach donned covetously one evening.

Most American males have, as do I, a selection of baseball type caps, each advertising an athletic team, automobile, farm implement, heavy equipment machine, or power tool. As favorite I waver between my green John Deere or the bright orange Ditch Witch versions. My sense of courtesy won't permit me to wear them at the dinner table.

Probably most conspicuous in the collection would be my well worn, or perhaps better said worn well, academic mortarboard. I have little occasion to wear it now, which is OK. My disquiet with the pomposity posed by professorial parades has eroded all sense of preeminence implied by academic regalia and mortarboards. Parading without my hat to pester the deans was a temptation to which I surrendered on occasion. It was a protest and momentary escape from the hubris.

My grandsons aren't queuing up for dibs on my gold-tasseled mortarboard.

JANUARY 14

Reflections

The visage that stared back at me from the bathroom mirror this morning startled me. It seemed more wizened than I had remembered. I don't mean to infer that it had been some time since I paid any attention to the images reflected there. It is possible that today my gaze may have lingered too long. Examining the reflection is, I am quite certain, a ritual performed daily by all who live with a mirror, myself included.

I think no other image, real or imagined, carries as much freight as those reflected by our mirrors. A mirror can evoke the entire gamut of human emotion. A mirror can be unrealistically flattering or brutally but honestly critical. Few there are who can view themselves in a mirror with total objectivity. It is in the mirror where self-esteem collides with self-image, where vanity and reality clash. My self-image and the one in the mirror have scuffled there. I don't intend to detail my in-front-of-the-mirror encounters with myself and risk exposing my emotional eccentricities other than to say that most of the time my mirror has been kind to me.

Why then this reflection about images? The wizened visage, which startled me this morning, caused me wonder how it got that way. Upon reflection it occurs to me that all of the countless images that have flashed before me in my mirror have been superimposed into the fused image I saw this morning.

There is history hidden in that countenance.

JANUARY 16

Recovering

Have you noticed that all retired people after a certain age start to look retired? One doesn't look like a retired banker, or a retired carpenter, or a retired professor, or retired anything. One just looks retired. It's inevitable. People can no longer tell what you did for a living just by looking at you.

When that happens people begin to ask, "And what did you do for a living?" I say, "I was a professor for forty years." Apologetically they say, "Oh, I'm sorry. Have you recovered yet?" Getting over being a professor may be something one never gets over, but I have been working at it.

I joined PA (Professors Anonymous), a small club of people trying to break addictions acquired in the professoriate— the most serious of which is talking too much. Here's how it works. When you are tempted or feel the urge to start pontificating or give a speech, call a club member with the hope they can talk you out of it.

As part of my recovery I decided to write a book, and while it doesn't always work out that way, books like speeches should be about something. And that something ought to be something about which the writer-speaker knows something. So I decided to write about professors, the one subject about which I should know something. I began by assuming that exposing the fantasies and foibles of the professoriate would expedite my restoration, but that didn't help. I still am vulnerable to the invitation to make a speech. >>>

The invitation to give a speech is seductive, especially for professors whose major activity is or has been talking. Until now I have had some success in resisting, but for the first time since retirement I agreed to speak. I got tricked into this — I succumbed to flattery. An invitation to speak in public carries with it the flattering innuendo that you have something to say. That is tough to resist.

Hello, my name is Howard, and I am a recovering professor.

JANUARY 17

Affirmation

During a recent return to the task of culling my collection of professional documents and files left over from duty in the academic trenches, I discovered a research paper written during a sabbatical leave near the end of my professorial tenure. As I reread the forgotten paper I was reminded of the circumstances that motivated the study.

Having observed some growing dissatisfaction among many of my younger colleagues, I strayed beyond the edges of my professional expertise and spent a semester studying the research on the psychology of work behavior—especially the expectations of workers pertaining to motivation and compensation. The professional literature reported widespread discontent among workers about the absence of personal affirmation or recognition as individuals of worth beyond their job performance.

My experience with affirmation from my superiors (a dubious category) has been quite spotty. In fact, none of them ever acknowledged my report to them about my study. It was, borrowing Emily Dickinson's words, *my letter to the world who never wrote to me.*

But my life has never been devoid of affirmation, the sort of confirmation that matters. It is the pats on the back and the hugs that come divested of all expectation of reward that count. The assurance of Pat's enduring and endearing affirmation during our six-decade journey together has been inestimable. Our daughters' estimation of my worthiness may be a bit inflated, but I can live with that. In our grandchildren's words, we are the 'Grand Guys.' What marvelous perception! And, of course, there are the persistent, priceless unspoken expressions of worth by friends and colleagues, which have no context other than mutual respect and unconditional affection.

My most cherished words of affirmation were spoken by granddaughter Kyrsten one Sunday morning. That we were on the way to church may have turned the child's mind to thoughts of greatness. Having been taught by her mother to direct unanswerable questions to me on the premise that "he knows all that stuff" Kyrsten announced to her brother Jordan, "I know somebody who knows everything."

"I do too. It's God," Jordan replied.

"Oh, yes, Him too." Kyrsten said. Of course, Krysten now grown has learned I am not in that league.

But being near the top, if only momentarily, is unforgettable.

JANUARY 22

A Song

I went to church today, which is not unusual inasmuch as Sunday is the day I normally go to church. I am often nagged by the thought that my participation in this weekly ritual may be as much habit as it is devotion. But that is not all this piece is about.

Today we sang a song, which is not unusual either inasmuch as we generally sing songs. Some Sundays we sing more songs than I think is necessary. However, that judgment is not mine to make and I am grateful. Unfortunately, it is incredibly easy to allow unsavory (sinful) thoughts to mar our attempts to worship. For example, silently critiquing the choices others prefer in their attempts to sing praises. But that is not all this is about either.

This is about a song we sang today. The song was written by a talented friend, beautiful in person and spirit. She declares that the song was given to her by God. I believe God works mysteriously and I can't imagine God giving this song to anyone else. It is as beautiful as the woman who created it.

I confess I didn't sing as much as listened. I was overwhelmed not only by the exquisite beauty of the song but was distracted by reminisces of the way the song came to be. It is a song brief in its words but infinite in its scope. The music is contagious and the text captures the essence of worship like no other song I sing. And it thrust me into an extraordinarily profound awareness of the presence of God. >>>

I didn't know a song could do that. Maybe they all can and it is I who won't let them.

JANUARY 23

Reciprocity

Several years ago I had the honor of eulogizing a popular, ninety-three-year-old rancher friend. Jim was a friendly neighbor, successful cattleman, church and community leader with scores of friends and admirers. His son, with whom I chatted later, lamented what seemed to him a scarcity of folks assembled to memorialize his father. He had momentarily forgotten that at 93 his father had outlived many, if not most, of his friends at whose memorializing he was probably present. But I think I understand his disappointment.

Last week the local newspaper announced the passing of four people, all of whom had been colleagues or associates of ours at the academic institution where we spent most of our professional lives. All of these folks were well into the decade of life indicated by the Psalmist as the final years of earthly sojourn and had arrived at the stop sign at the end of the exit lane. There is no green light there.

One obvious consequence of the demise of friends, in addition to the attendant sense of loss, is the decision whether to attend the final service—a decision that confronts us oldsters with increasing frequency. I doubt that I am the only one who struggles with that determination. But am I the only one who wonders whether the deceased would have come to my farewell? Of course, I know there's no getting even with those who didn't attend your memorial service.

Attendance at memorial services cannot be reciprocal.

JANUARY 24
Different

Rachel was my younger sister and the last born of our family of seven children. January 24 is the anniversary of her birth and when that day of January reappears in the annual cycle of days, my thoughts about her linger in ways profoundly different from the reminiscences of my other siblings on their birthdays. You see, Rachel was different.

She arrived at our cold, Minnesota farmhouse on this day in 1933. She weighed a mere four pounds, not the hardy eight-pound-plus birth weights of the rest of us. The novelty of a very small baby diminished quickly when it became apparent to us kids that all was not well with her. My mother refused to countenance the doctor's diagnosis that Rachel was congenitally defective and that she should, in the best interest of the family, be institutionalized. While desperately searching for some explanation that would absolve her of the blame for the child's defects, she vowed never to abandon her child.

We lived with the guilt and shame imposed on us by society's blatant stigma attending families with imperfect children. Although, as an adult formally educated in genetics, I can talk objectively about the unfortunate misalignment of chromosomes and the attending developmental consequences that are manifested in Down's Syndrome persons, I am still unable to reveal my thoughts, emotions, and efforts to distance myself from the situation back then. >>>

I was seven years old and, having been told that God answers prayers, I prayed as fervently as ever a boy could pray that God would fix the things that were wrong with my little sister. When I asked Mother why God didn't answer my prayers, she said, "There is nothing wrong with Rachael. She is just different."

When family and friends were gathered to memorialize Rachel's life I was suddenly startled by the realization that my prayers had been selfishly more for me than they were for her. Fix my little sister and the disquiet in my life will go away.

That still troubles me, especially on the 24th of January.

JANUARY 26

It's Not Funny

It is often said of oldsters when they appear to be a bit confused that they are losing it. What the *it* they are said to be losing is usually unstated, but there is little ambivalence about it. It is generally understood to mean they have begun to loose their grip on total awareness of what is going on both in and outside their heads. Not infrequently such observations convey a sense of amusement. While it is seldom said in the presence of one who has grown a bit unsure about immediate circumstances, it is a hurtful thing to say and I have resolved not to do that.

There are several aspects of this manifestation of aging about which I have become a bit curious, however. I do wonder whether folks who are manifesting this malady know that they are, in fact, losing it and should be alerted.

I don't know anyone over eighty (myself included) who doesn't know that they are old and getting older. Various aches and physical limitations, as well as one's mirror, keep one informed. But the mirror does not monitor subtle changes in behavior.

I am not concerned about the increase in the time it takes to recall the name of someone I have known forever. I have had 18-year-old students who couldn't remember the name of the large bone in their leg long enough to write it on the blank of a test. But I would be concerned if I couldn't remember what an object is or who a person is. I know folks to whom that has happened. It is one thing to forget; it's another not to know you have forgotten. That's a frightful loss about which nothing is funny.

So why should I be amused when I found the coffee I intended to reheat in the refrigerator?

JANUARY 27

Genes, Generations, and Gratitude

An increasingly common feature in local newspapers, along with pictures of centenarians, are photographs picturing persons representing four or five generations. All of which speaks to the lengthening life span of our citizens. All of our children, their children, and their children's children gathered at Gramom's house during the recent holiday season and posed with us for one of these multigenerational portraits. It's my house too, but that fact seems to be overshadowed by the warm welcoming hospitality so graciously manifested by Pat—mother, grandmother, great grandmother par excellence. The dynamics of the group were fascinating to observe. Observer was my major assignment.

Our gang members seemed to enjoy the mix. They all were true to their roles. The youngest grandchildren impatient for independence want to be like their college-age siblings. The adult grandchildren, grown tall enough to look down at us, still look up to us as icons of wisdom and integrity. Our great-grandchildren are content with their status. Our children in the fast lanes are creatively, courageously, and optimistically making their way in this tumultuous world. And like us, watch and wonder at it all. But the sociology of the gathering is not what this is about. It's about the genes of the gang.

With practiced objectivity I monitored the mixing, matching, and manifestation of genes in the founding gene pool, a side effect of my professional participation in the science of genetics. I charted the expression of genes for eye-color, ear lobe shape, relative finger length, premature graying, musical and writing talent. One interesting genetically influenced talent that has not been diluted by the intrusion of genes from in-law gene pools is the ability to roll one's tongue. A number of us still proudly demonstrate that dexterity, which we do sensitively not to suggest superiority.

Mostly I am awed by the potential of genetic mechanisms, whether natural or divine, to create beautiful, uncountable, one-of-a-kind persons. There were seventeen of us here, all of whom have fared well in this great gene roulette given the chips available to them.

Something about which we are grateful.

JANUARY 28

After Work

A local college student called to ask if he could interview Pat and me about the verities of retirement. I wondered about his interest in retirement. He is in a bit of hurry, I thought; he is only nineteen. It was an assignment for a course in journalism. We agreed and he arrived this evening, notebook and pen in hand, ready to hear our spin on this geriatric nebulosity in which we oldsters are assumed to be engaged.

I toyed with him a bit, mostly to alert him that our take on retirement didn't mesh well with the stereotypes commonly associated with pensioneering. The phenomenon of retirement conjures notions of Medicare and Social Security dependency, housing options with elders clustered or sequestered in huge housing complexes, expensive villas adjacent to golf courses. While people retire these days at increasingly younger ages, I suspect that retirees are generally stereotyped as aged, geezerly, curmudgeonly, frail and cranky. If they drive, the car will probably be a Buick.

Even though I am well beyond the mean age of retirees (especially if the range is determined by AARP membership), I refuse to be identified with either the golfers or the geezers. Curmudgeons maybe. I don't want to know about pills, pains or pathologies. Nor am I am impressed by how much one has traveled. I think of myself as one who, while no longer distracted by career or profession, continues to live in ways that nurture the mind, nourish the body, and nudge the soul.

If that's retirement, I have nailed it.

JANUARY 31
Get Over It

One aspect of language that has long intrigued me is the use of idioms—combinations of words the meanings of which cannot necessarily be ascertained from the meanings of the individual words. Common expressions like *on the ball, over the hill, kept in stitches, get on with it,* and *over my dead body* are familiar to most people, literate and illiterate alike. Idioms are a challenge for most people learning a new language. I am confident that some scholar somewhere has written seriously or otherwise about the phenomenon.

Why, I am not sure, but there is one idiom that has been banging around in my head lately. It could be that, like many of the notions that rattle around in my mind, it has something to do with the subliminal sense of diminishing future, which I believe is not uncommon in the minds of thoughtful oldsters. It could also be because the expression implies activity that generally requires time. The idiom of which I am thinking is *get over it!*

Getting over stuff is not easy for elders whose practices and preferences (alliteration is one of mine) are firmly entrenched. The habits of seniors are often thought by younger folks to impede progress. A friend who once registered his disquiet about the lack of sophistication in popular, contemporary church music was told by the minister of youth to *get over it*. >>>

Some things cannot be 'gotten over' easily, if at all, like having been named Howard. But then that is seldom a problem for people not named Howard. Getting over being old is another circumstance that takes more time than many of us had thought. Getting over cancer also tends to be difficult, especially for older folks. Although a friend of mine did recently. He died.

Getting over his happy presence will take time.

February

FEBRUARY 2

A Premonition

Children are often asked what they want to be when they get big—that is, grow up. The onetime favorites for boys of fireman or policeman may have been replaced by rock star or professional athlete. I haven't asked a child the question lately.

Professor was not on my boyhood list of things I wanted to be when I grew up. Professors simply were not part of the drought and depression-stricken real world in which I lived as a boy in the dirty thirties. My father was a farmer. I wanted to be a farmer. My Danish immigrant grandfather was also a farmer. He had names for all of his grandchildren, names other than those assigned by their parents. He called me "the perfesser." I remember being envious of my brother whom he called "the truck driver."

"Be a perfesser," my grandfather would say in his delightful Danish accent. "It beats working for a living. It's nice clean inside work and, apart from some weighty ideas, there's no heavy lifting." No one else ever said to me, "Be a professor." Although a disgruntled student once said to me, "Did it ever occur to you that you should not be a professor?"

Why my grandfather called me "the perfesser" I will never know. It didn't occur to me to ask him. I often wonder, now that I have retired and have time to think about it. There was no hint in my childhood or teenage years that I was destined to be one. That possibility absolutely never crossed my mind.

I wanted to be a farmer and given my immigrant parents' old-world traditions about sons following their fathers' vocations, no one ever discouraged that aspiration. Not even my grandfather, who continued to call me "the perfesser" (a title I did not understand). I wish I'd had occasion or the boldness to ask him. I prefer to think it was because I displayed some precocious talent for argument or abstraction. Surely, it was not because I talked too much.

Ironically, among my grandfather's twenty-eight grandchildren I was the only one who attempted farming.

Interestingly, I was also the only professor.

FEBRUARY 3

The Other End

One of my favorite leisure pursuits is playing with words, an activity probably carried over from professional days trafficking in ideas, the major commodity of which is words. Like most folks who have spent a life in the domain of ideas, I have developed an awareness of words. With a bit of immodesty, I admit, I think of myself as a connoisseur of words.

Not infrequently I am surprised by the power and utility of little words. Today the word that refuses to stay out of my musing is the uncommonly common word *end*. And I swear that this momentary obsession with *end* has nothing to do with my travels in the exit lane.

It doesn't require great wisdom to realize that no event, place, or thing can be understood apart from either its origin or termination. Ends are ubiquitous. I suppose beginnings are as well, but that's not what this is about.

Apart from literal ends, the notion of ends permeates figurative speech—in the end, end of the day, end of the rope, end of the road, and of course, loose ends. There is one of these expressions with both literal and figurative allusions that lingers in the forefront today—it is *the other end*.

Just having removed the ashes from our wood-burning stove, my thoughts turned to boyhood days when our family heated our big, old, cold farmhouse with firewood mostly sawn by hand. Many winter days arriving home from school I would see my father sawing logs for firewood with a long unwieldy cross-cut saw.

"Grab your mittens and take the other end," he would say. It was hard work made easier by his encouragement and instruction. "Don't press the saw, let its weight do the work," I was advised. While envying my brothers inside by the warm fire, I was proud (more in retrospect perhaps) to have been chosen to be at the other end of a memorable experience with my Dad.

Pat and I are nearing a significant passage in our decades of honoring vows to love and cherish each other forever. Sixty years ago we agreed to some promises, made extraordinarily easy for me because of Pat's rare combination of grace and beauty both in person and spirit. I don't know which of us has been at the other end of all this, but I got the best deal.

To have been at the other end of a very good thing is a very good thing!

FEBRUARY 4

Who?

It is safe to say that most humans are at some time or other bewildered about the mystery and meaning of existence. It is also true that in this contemporary culture of self-analysis with its attending psychobabble we are encouraged, in the name of good mental health, to indulge in some self-searching or searching for one's self. Psychologists exploiting the self-awareness instinct in all humans undoubtedly perpetrate that urging.

We hear and read accounts of personal effort to find themselves. Pat, who usually arises earlier than I, often greets me with: "Did you sleep well?" Or "Are you up for all day?" Or as she did this AM, "How did you find yourself this morning?" to which I replied, "I just threw back the covers and there I was."

But it's not that easy. All this nattering about achieving some comfort with oneself is confusing because of the premium society places on the status one has achieved in the meritocracy of our culture. I can't recall the number of times I have been identified as a professor or a biologist, which doesn't distinguish me from countless other persons who are also professors or biologists. That is not who I am; that's what I do. And doing biology tells me little about myself that being a farmer didn't tell me.

Oh, I know that context or association has much to do with the answer to the question, "Who am I?" The fact that I was

359

born a twin to Scandinavian immigrant parents, one of seven siblings, married to Pat, father of Suzanne and Beth certainly identify me apart from all the unfortunate folks who were not any of those.

Being totally human (contrary to the conclusions of some students) I have put in my time pondering the who-am-I puzzle. I am content to say with Popeye the Sailorman, "I yam what I yam." In fact, if I weren't, I would certainly be envious of whoever was.

My current and quite comforting answer to the question is: I am only a sinner saved by grace.

FEBRUARY 5

Too Few Words

Among the hundreds of students in whose education I was privileged to participate, there are dozens who have stayed or returned to town to seek their professional fortunes. It is not uncommon for me to encounter physicians, dentists, lawyers, nurses, teachers and even biology professors who attended my classes. I still indulge myself with the fantasy that I had something to do with their successes.

I am often amazed by the memories that surface when by chance I meet them on the street, in church, or in their offices. Last week a former student friend stopped by to announce his return to the city to continue his dental practice. During his student years he was a pleasant, somewhat boyish, clean-cut young fellow. As he entered my classroom one afternoon obviously disturbed, he proclaimed loudly in words well beyond the line that separates youthful impetuosity and the constraints of maturity that he was pissed off. I was offended. I had been in the military when that expression was invented as a way of expressing extreme disquiet, but even among seasoned soldiers it was considered too vulgar for polite, mixed company. This lapse of civility, as I perceived it, precipitated a lecture on my hope that his college education might provide him a vocabulary with which he could express his feelings in good taste. He says that is the only one of my lectures he remembers.

It was then, as I recall, when vulgarity began to slip into the media, both print and video, and was readily adopted by young people. Why should it be otherwise when the film industry employs the f-word without restraint? It is ironic that the word, despite its use even by preadolescents, is considered too vulgar for use in print.

You may wonder why this degeneration of civility should matter to me, now far down the road. I am not too old to be offended. It has nothing to do with intolerance, although intolerance about some matters is not wrong. Some indignant intolerance along the way by adults surely might have made a difference. Could this demise have begun with us?

I wonder what words are off limits for the dentist's kids.

FEBRUARY 6

Nuptial Harmony

That opposites attract is a well-known adage. It is true that opposite electro-magnetic charges have easily demonstrated strong attraction. The extent to which the attraction of other opposites is universal is uncertain and often debated. There are those who insist that the greater the differences between two humans, the stronger the bond or attraction will be. Current political activity clearly demonstrates the nonsense of that.

In the matter of matrimony, some folks argue that differences of all sorts between two individuals enhance the congeniality of the couple. Not so, say the experts—compatibility thrives on likenesses in attitude, tastes, values, education, aspiration, expectation, self-esteem, and experience.

Recently Pat and I marked a significant passage in our long, pleasant, and remarkably compatible life together. My dictionary defines our relationship as companionate, a word, although not necessarily sophisticated, that says it all. It means right for each other. How could we have known that? Much of what we know about each other that gives truth to the word we learned after we were married. None of it has to do with the notion of opposites with one exception. We are quite aware of the real physical attraction of gender opposites.

It turns out, either serendipitously or providentially, we were indeed right for each other. We were both raised on marginally productive midwestern farms by families strongly identified with old-world religious and culinary heritages. We both enjoyed the affirmation and embrace of extended families. We enjoyed the perks of rural living and endured the hardships of droughts, depression and world war. We both were taken to school by horse and sleigh. With family support, we both began our move to independence immediately after high school— Pat in college and I in the military. We, perhaps immodestly, believed we were more mature and realistic about marriage than most of today's twenty-one-year-olds.

Our culinary experiences and preferences with one exception were much alike. Our families' wholesome meals were made from garden grown vegetables, wild berries and fruit, poultry and dairy products. We were at ease with turnips, parsnips, and rutabaga. There was one minor, perhaps, but real contrast with the potential to disrupt our nuptial harmony. Early on a couple of ethnic delicacies quite foreign to our respective culinary preferences emerged as unexpected incompatibilities. My Scandinavian parents taught us to savor the tactile and taste subtleties of lutefisk—fish sun-dried and preserved in a briny unconventional gelatinizing solution. Pat learned to relish the gustatatory and olfactory sensations of sauerkraut— cabbage fermented in its own juice and brine. These savory extremes were quite foreign from our respective cuisines. But we resolved not to allow a bit of sour cabbage or adulterated fish compromise our culinary compatibility

We married 'for better or worse' and live on in expanded culinary harmony.

FEBRUARY 8

Ogling

Our city's annual International Auto Show began today. That it is billed as an international event amuses me a bit. Our modest airport (Spokane International) serves air traffic to and from Canada, which may contribute to the notion that our car show merits global status. Except for a few folks from nearby Canada, I don't think many non-nationals attend. Of course, I know that many automobiles are produced by international automakers, which probably justifies the billing. My mildly pejorative disquiet about the marquee didn't preclude my participation in this community ogling of new cars, most of which were priced beyond the reach of 90% of the crowd including me.

Being a self-acclaimed connoisseur of new automobiles I strolled through the exhibits coveting many new models, I confess—especially the racy two-seaters, which Pat had advised me to ignore with the argument that we were far beyond the age where a convertible would bolster our self-image. "It's too late," she said.

Growing weary of inspecting automobiles I couldn't have and didn't need, I entertained myself by observing the crowd of oglers, who were still pursuing their fantasies. There were serious shoppers conspicuously shaking hands with smiling salesmen. Wealthy ranchers in western hats at the Cadillac display. Young couples lost in their dreams, vulnerable to the hype. Macho twenty-something guys in need of a self-image boost drooling over the obscenely outsized Hummers and pickups. Senior citizen couples, whose current cars will likely outlast them, enjoying an inexpensive outing. I can imagine other crowd watchers including me in that bunch.

I brought home my usual collection of brochures to read at leisure to stay informed about options to sustain my new car fantasies until next year.

I auto know better.

FEBRUARY 9

Untied

A few days ago a request came from a rancher friend of ours asking me to officiate at the service memorializing his 93-year-old mother. Loma and her husband, Charles, were cherished friends whom Pat and I came to know 36 years ago when we served as lay ministers in their small, rural, community church. Loma was a good and gracious woman who deserved all the respect, admiration, honor, and accolades due a departed saint. My assignment was easy.

The real challenge came as I was readying myself for the event. I had grown lax in attention to my sartorial impressions. I, along with my professorial cohorts, had long abandoned sartorial respectability as a prerequisite for addressing a college class. Careless casualness (jeans, sandals and no socks) had become the norm. Think students setting the dress code for professors.

This sartorial indifference has invaded sanctuaries of worship. I remember a time when saving one's best for God meant dressing in all the finery one's budget and pride would permit. Even clergymen have abandoned dressing their best for God. My concession to casual church attire has been to discard my necktie. It had been months since I'd tied one on.

But Loma deserved my very best and to attend her farewell, much less speak untied—so to speak, was not an option. Much to my dismay, however, I could not tie my tie. It wasn't only that my once dexterous fingers were no longer nimble. My memory of the procedure was simply absent, a dreadfully scary circumstance for a near elderly guy like me. Who would rescue me? Certainly not my neighborhood grandson, untied since birth.

After some trial and error, I managed a beautifully symmetrical double Windsor four-in-hand knot. One of my best!

I like to believe Loma would have been pleased.

FEBRUARY 11

Little Old Man

Throughout most of my life I have had a thing about being short. Actually, I don't think of myself as being short. But in the context of four tall brothers I came to view myself as not tall. This rather personal disquiet had its onset at the beginning. My twin brother was a quarter-inch longer at birth than I, and I never outgrew the disparity. He was always at least an inch and a half taller than I, and the younger brothers ranged from one to four inches taller. I always had to stand in the front row in the family photographs. I privately contended with the inequity of it all by assuming an aura of intellectual superiority, which they willingly conceded because it never showed in the pictures.

Now I contend with a generation of nephews six-foot two-inches or more, the tallest of which is six-foot seven. And you guessed it, a basketball player. Not only that, but all three of my grandsons are, as the contemporary jargon says it, way taller than I. It seems that being the shortest is another one of those things one never gets over.

You may wonder what all this nattering about height has to do with travels in the exit lane. No one attentive to age-related changes (in oneself as well as in fellow sojourners) can miss the diminution of stature in oldsters taking 'at bats' in extra innings. Incidentally, we are alerted to the phenomenon early. Fairy tales and children stories introduce the notion of little old men. I am not aware of a tale that embraces a tall old man. >>>

A reminder of this downward trend was imposed on me by the nurse during a recent appointment with my doctor (a tall fellow). "Take off your boots (my western boots have high heels) and stand by the wall," she commanded. As she recorded the measurement, to my chagrin, she announced it loudly to the entire waiting room. I won't reveal what it was because it isn't any of your business, but it was inches less than I have been content to believe.

Still wounded by that experience, I wandered to campus to hear a public lecture. In the foyer I encountered a former colleague whom I had not seen recently, a fellow at one time taller than I and a bit younger but approaching the exit lane. To my surprise, I stood eye-to-eye with Joe. I hope I didn't seem overly glad to notice his diminution.

By the way, I had put my boots back on.

FEBRUARY 12

Dream Come True

Most of the nation was hysterical with anticipation today. The jackpot of the multi-state lottery reached a record $365,000,000 and millions of tickets were sold each minute, one of which was mine. I still have it. Ordinarily I don't publicize my gambling capers. That is not because I don't wish to be found morally wanting by my more virtuous friends, nor is it because I don't want to be thought ignorant of the minuscule probability of carrying off the prize. It's one of those things that fall into the realm of nobody's business. I believe I reside within the limits of emotional fitness, which permits some serious, healthy fantasy. The adrenalin rush that attends the thought of suddenly becoming unimaginably wealthy certainly energizes the dreams of this pragmatic veteran.

I went to sleep with my $1 ticket under my pillow (I bought just one chance with the rationale that it is the least one can do to win) and drifted into dreams of what my millions might do for me and my family, sleepily presuming that certainly God would agree that my family is worthy of some good fortune. The whole bailiwick—new cars, new homes, education, debt-free careers, travel, leisure—all the luxuries my sleep-muddled mind associated with wealth.

Even in my fitful nocturnal stupor, however, it occurred to me that a fortune of that enormity brings serious stewardship responsibilities. What about the multitudes of poor, sick, repressed people? Would I willingly give it all away? Then I fell into deep sleep, un-dreaming sleep, the sort that psychologists claim un-muddles the mind and settles the soul.

I dreamed again. The essence of that dream was that I didn't win the lottery. Ever awaken with the startling realization that your dream had come true? Except for the dollar, I was back where I started from, which is usually the case.

Folks should be cautious about what they dream, especially oldsters. What eighty year-old guy has time to spend $365,000,000?

FEBRUARY 13

Looking Good

It must have been the new model brochures I gathered at the auto show last week and fell asleep reading last night that caused me to waken reminiscing about cars I have known. Since I was a kid at the edge of the horse and buggy days, I have been intrigued by cars. My grandfather, who lived with us his later years, never owned nor drove an automobile. His personal transportation was a handsome buggy and two sorrel ponies. He presented a striking image in that rig. I vaguely remember riding with him, but I do fondly recall Molly, one of the ponies that became ours (my brothers and mine) when Granddad died. We drove Molly and the remnants of his old buggy to school our final year at the neighborhood country school.

My first automobile ride, although I scarcely remember it, was in my mother's 1917 Dodge touring car purchased with her schoolteacher salary. My mother taught my father to drive. Our family cars were a 1928 Essex, a 1926 Buick Master, and a 1929 Ford Model A, which we drove to high school on occasion. The last car registered to my parents was a 1936 Ford, purchased with money primarily from the wages of my brothers and me.

I remember the heady post-war days when automobiles became the focus of our culture's way of life. While I confess to some fantasizing, fortunately I never surrendered to the need to boost my ego with an expensive muscle car. An eager salesman once said to me, "Wow, you sure look good in that convertible." I agreed and replied, "I am sure that's true, but it's not the car. I'd look good in any car—even used cars." He went on to another customer who apparently needed the boost. I saw that guy driving the convertible later in the day.

Pat and I have not been slothful in our support of the auto industry. We have owned several new autos, always appropriate to our station in life. I will admit, however, that in later years I have been quite intentional about avoiding the geezerly image that attends old guys driving Buicks.

In fact, I paused this morning by our new Honda for a few seconds of silent gratitude,

FEBRUARY 14

Excuses

Certain days on society's calendar are marked as days when it is appropriate, expected in fact, for one to buy gifts. Christmas, of course, is major among these gift-giving opportunities. Easter bunnies and baskets have adulterated Easter so that children grow up expecting chocolate eggs, oblivious about the truth of the season. Mother's Day, Father's Day, and now (due to extended longevity) Grandparent's Day remind us that there are folks who deserve a card or gift. Prior to all of these special days we are so barraged with reminders not to miss an opportunity or obligation to contribute to the economic well being of card printers, candy makers, and florists that the intent of the event is obscured. Halloween is another one. Lots of candy is requisite for kids on Halloween.

And then there is St. Valentine's Day. I object to the myth so extensively perpetrated by society that we need a day giving us permission to say, "I love you" to those God has given us to love. One shouldn't need excuses or reasons to say overtly, "I love you." To do so is good for the soul, both hers and mine. Even so, there are folks like the gnarled old farmer who was heard to say, "I love my wife so much it is all I can do to keep from telling her." Could it be that Valentine's Day was conceived with guys like him in mind?

Through 60 Valentine seasons Pat and I have been quite casual about any emphasis on the day. We have managed remarkably well, I believe, to effectively express our mutual affection without any prompting from society. However, thinking one Valentine dinner certainly wouldn't mar my reputation as an independent thinker, I planned to surprise Pat with an invitation to our favorite restaurant, totally aware of the possibility that the surprise might cause her to think I had done something wrong. Unfortunately, my penchant to procrastinate precluded my securing a reservation. The prime times were all booked by romantics whose motives are not for me to critique.

We settled for hors d'oeuvres and libation at a delightful bistro and left convinced, reasons or excuses notwithstanding, that celebrating love is a good thing to do.

Next year I will make reservations early.

FEBRUARY 15

My Numbers

It is truly ironic that in this self-assigned exercise of numbering my days my identity is characterized by a catalog of numbers. I have two official government issued numbers that are mine alone. One is my military service number, 1711820 assigned to me when at seventeen I enlisted in the U.S. Army Air Corps. Why I so clearly remember that number is a mystery. The other, of course, is my Social Security number, which I have never learned and which I can't reveal here lest thieves steal my identity. Why anyone would want my identity puzzles me. I have little (very little) money and have no distinguishing physical features that would cause flight attendants to move me to first class or that would arouse suspicion from security people. I am not even tall. But don't misunderstand me. I am proud of who I am.

All of my official records show me as a white, American citizen born 04-11-26. That doesn't distinguish me, however. The same was true of my twin brother, but my S.S. number changes that. It is in my medical records where my individuality begins to emerge. I have blood pressure numbers, cholesterol numbers, LDL & HDL numbers, PSA levels, BG levels, CRP, and A1C numbers. There may be more, but I don't get to read the doctor's book (now a computer file). In fact, when my doc calls he seldom asks how I am. He asks instead, "What are your numbers?" My response is, "You tell me—you have the book." He reports, "Your numbers look good and your A1C is 7.0."

I can live with that.

FEBRUARY 17

Good Guys

Resolved not to drift apart or squander opportunities to stay close during our overtime years, Pat and I do more tasks together. When we were farmers Pat did the household chores and I the barnyard chores. While teaching and raising children we worked with a mutually accepted and respected division of labor and we frequently spelled each other. But now I find myself more and more engaged in what was at one time considered 'women's work'—washing windows, cooking, vacuuming carpets, laundry, and grocery shopping. Routinely I accompany Pat on the latter, a regular and indispensable outing. She considers pricing and makes choices. I get to drive the grocery cart. Occasionally Pat lets me choose which cart to drive. All the wheels should want to go in the same direction, she says.

Today, as we were moving about our favorite Safeway store, I arrived at an intersection of aisles when another chap, whose wife was letting him drive, arrived precisely at the same moment. In the seconds of deciding who should pass first, the other driver said, "Hey, I know you. You're one of the good guys." Of course I stepped back and let him pass. Flattered by his assessment I wondered what had been his first clue. Later when he entered the checkout line two places ahead of me, I realized I had already been checked out.

Good guys don't always finish first.

FEBRUARY 18

Keeping Busy

During one's productive years one is seldom asked, "What are you doing these days?" It is generally understood that working folks are busy with their careers, which circumscribes much of their activities. After a query about ones health, the question about one's busyness is the next-most-frequent inquiry directed at pensioners. I suppose it's a fair and well-meaning question, yet I struggle for answers that don't appear brusque.

When I perceive the inquiry is largely ceremonial and the questioner is not seriously concerned about whether I am carrying my weight, I usually say, "I am staying out of the way" or "Just hanging out." Both, I believe, are respectable things for oldsters to be doing and a conclusion to which a lot of older folks have already come.

If I suspect the quizzer is anxious for some serious conversation, I might say, "Nothing." That is not to say I ignore the question, which I think would be discourteous. I often quickly add the comment that doing nothing is quite different from not doing anything.

That sort of nit-picking distinction is a carry-over from ideological battles in the professoriate. People who enjoy sparring about meaningless distinctions in phraseology (like practicing intellectuals) who have the need to display their rhetorical prowess will want to know what the difference between doing nothing and not doing anything really is. I could point out that *doing* (even if it is nothing one is doing) has a positive sense to it, whereas *not doing* could suggest idleness or negligence, not generally considered to be virtuous.

My answer to the question is, of course, "I don't have the foggiest idea, but thinking about it keeps me off the street and out of the way and leaves the impression that I actually am doing something."

I think my wage earner friends would be pleased.

FEBRUARY 19

Baptism

There probably are persons who have absolutely no concept of the ritual of baptism. There are others whose notions about the practice are vague and whose indifference about it is deep. But for persons for whom matters of faith are significant, baptism is a vital component of their belief systems. The formal procedures of the ritual are as diverse as the groups who perform them. I know—I have witnessed countless baptisms.

The decisions about when one should be baptized are more frequently not made by the one being baptized. Whether individuals should be baptized as children or as persons adult enough to understand what's going on has not been given to me to decide. However, the latter seems more defensible to me.

All of this is preamble to my observations of a baptism I witnessed today—an extraordinarily moving scenario. Dave, a professional colleague and friend of forty years, knelt humbly at an altar to be baptized at the age of seventy. He is an intelligent, accomplished scientist, thoughtful about matters of faith, acutely aware of both the spiritual and material subtleties of the natural world, a man of unquestioned integrity, at times a bit arrogant and independent, but always kind and gentle to his family and friends. Here he was kneeling meekly before his friends in a remarkable public act of submission and commitment to the God of creation and now the God of redemption. Dave had given long and serious thought to this event. It was his decision to do this. He understands what it is all about.

A babe represents the potential of life. It takes a lifetime to embrace its mysteries.

FEBRUARY 20

My Mirror and Me

Contemplation of the concept of self and its relationship to the biological stuff of which we are made continues to be an intellectual obsession of mine. That is, it still lingers in the jumble of ideas that joust for attention when my mind is free from tending to the routine business of remaining sane and staying alive.

Although there is no dearth of words discussing the existence or the nature of this entity within us and with which we seem to have conversations about ourselves, I don't intend this to be a discourse on any of that confabulation. I assume everyone has some notion about this phenomenon of thinking about oneself, especially as it is reflected in concepts like self-worth, self-esteem, self-image, self-doubt, self-discipline, self-denial, etcetera.

A lot of stuff about self ought to be self-evident, but I am not sure that is always true. Recently I have wondered why a guy who looks so good in the mirror can look so bad on photographs. Or why the mirror on the wall tells you something different from what your head tells you. One wonders whether one's mirror may be dishonest.

I have discovered my self-image has been evolving, which I submit is not only inevitable but the recognition of which is probably quite healthy. One's self-image ought to keep pace with changes in one's actual visage. That's not easy. Something gets in the way. >>>

I want to trust my mirror. It's been kind to me through the years, but perhaps it has not done as well distinguishing my self from the real me, as does the camera. Self is susceptible to flattery.

Oh, well, self-image not withstanding, sooner or later an old guy is going to see an old man in his mirror.

FEBRUARY 22

An Unfaithful Friend

Leslie was his name. He was our father's 'hired man,' the title assigned to young men who helped with the livestock chores and cultivation and harvest of field crops. Traditionally they lived and ate their meals with the families for whom they worked. Without the benefit of union protection they worked under the whims and goodwill of the farmer boss. I know. I worked as a hired man for three of my teenage summers.

We became pals, Leslie and I. He allowed me to tag along while he worked. He let me drive his team of horses in the hay fields and during the threshing season. Leslie was unlike most of the young men in the neighborhood who had been our hired men in earlier summers. He had been in the U.S. Navy. He knew city life, a domain quite foreign to rural Minnesota farm boys. He had been to Texas. And he had been in prison. He had been convicted of forgery, a new word in my vocabulary, the meaning and wrong of which was unclear.

That summer I learned about prison life and about parole. Parolees' movements were restricted. My Uncle Nels, the county sheriff who had arranged for Leslie to work for my father, visited regularly with Leslie. "Checking up on me," Leslie would say. I wasn't allowed to listen to his conversations with the sheriff, but I overheard Leslie assert that he wasn't going to spend another winter in Minnesota. >>>

Although I knew little about places other than Minnesota, I surmised the rational of Leslie's declaration.

Leslie was permitted to leave the farm and go into town on Saturday evenings—the major social meeting time of rural people. He was expected to be back to the farm by sun-up Sunday morning. My parents concern when he hadn't returned one Sunday morning was obvious. Some papers protruding from behind a mirror in Leslie's room revealed several check blanks on which Leslie had been perfecting my grandfather's signature. My grandfather, a Danish immigrant, wrote with a distinct old-European script. Leslie had perfected his signature. Now I knew what forgery was. With money from two twenty-dollar checks written on Granddad's account, Leslie was on his way to Texas.

Two weeks later the authorities apprehended him and returned him to the Minnesota penitentiary. His attempt to avoid another Minnesota winter had been thwarted. My parents received a letter apologizing for the hurt his escapade may have caused them. In my vague recollections the letter seemed less than an apology and more like an explanation of his caper.

It was not, as we assumed, an effort to escape winter in Minnesota. He simply found perfecting Grandfather's distinct Danish signature an irresistible challenge. The letter was signed in faultless, old-European script: Leslie Paulson, an unfaithful friend.

FEBRUARY 23

It Was Different Then

An eccentricity of mine is to think about what I have thinking about and then to wonder about it all. Recently I have been thinking again about growing up on that sand hill Minnesota farm during the drought and depression in the dirty thirties. Then, depression was something wrong with the economy and not with people. Most of the time we had no money. I thought that was because we were poor, not because the economy was depressed. I didn't even know the word economy then. I do remember the drought and the dust. But I don't remember being either happy or sad. We just were. I do remember being optimistic. It never occurred to me that things would not be better. Could it be that, as one gets older, times gone by are remembered as better than they were.

I have concluded that, although there may be good or bad days at any time in one's life, one should not think about time in terms of better or worse but rather as different. Now we have more than we did then. More convenient, but better? Then, we got along without electricity, plumbing, television, CDs, air-conditioning, cell phones, thermostats, and cruise control. We did have books and kerosene lamps to light the reading thereof.

We didn't have pre-school, nursery school or kindergarten. Those hadn't been invented yet, but I don't think I am worse off because of that. There were fewer stages of life then.

Adolescence hadn't been discovered yet and retirement was not something people did. President Roosevelt invented that along with Social Security and income taxes. I don't know whether those days were good or bad, but they were different.

Parenting was different then. My parents didn't have any helpful gadgets, but they managed. I doubt that they worried about their parenting skills. The word parenting didn't exist then either. My parents fed, clothed, loved, and cared for us without a lot of things that now seem essential, even without medical insurance. They went about raising kids without any awareness of an abstraction called parenting.

All of this is a lengthy preamble to what I would do if I were now caring for youngsters not yet twenty. I would marvel at the uniqueness of their individuality, observe with awe the development of their talents and potential, letting that proceed according to their awareness of themselves, and remind them when necessary that they live in the midst of others who have the same right to exist as they do. The only imperative I would impose upon myself would be the right to protect them from high-risk situations they might not recognize. Now that I think about it, that's what my parents did.

Perhaps things weren't so different after all.

FEBRUARY 25

The Off Ramp

Not all the thoughts that rumble through this oldster's mind are recollections of times gone by. Occasionally circumstances concentrate one's mental ramblings on probable, if not inevitable, scenarios.

For the past several weeks our streets and sidewalks have continuously been coated with ice. Staying upright is a challenge for young and old alike. Conditions like this tend to arrange folks in two categories: persons who have fallen and persons who are going to. Fallen young people generally get up, shaken perhaps, but fortunately unhurt. They may sport crutches or display casts, the latter emblazoned with the autographs of peers. Alerted to the treachery of icy surfaces they heal quickly, usually spared lingering debilitating consequences.

For fragile oldsters it's another story. We extra-inning folks learn vicariously that falling on the ice or falling for any other reason will quite likely shorten one's jaunt along the exit lane. A slip on the ice (or tripping over a rug) too frequently marks the point at which the exit lane becomes the off-ramp. Anyone attentive to contingencies of advanced age is aware of the potential for a mishap to hurry the demise of even the sturdiest of us old-timers.

We worry about Bill, our ninety-year-old friend, who just last week slipped and fell on the ice. It wasn't the first time that happened to him, but unfortunately, it may likely be the last.

I don't think I am obsessed with the imminent approach of the off-ramp, but I am definitely fixated on the icy spots.

FEBRUARY 26

What Matters

In his memoirs Henry Kissinger wrote that what mattered was "whether what one did in life made a difference." Difference can be defined so that the lives of the vast majority of citizens have not nor ever will make a difference. One might also wonder to whom the difference would matter. I have often wondered how many citizens, aware of the statement, examined their lives searching for differences they were making. All of this, however, is confabulation, serving mostly as fodder for intellectual discourse.

At the time of Kissinger's declaration, I was deep into my scramble for significance in the academy. I had already come to realize that just having been said did not necessarily make a proposition true. Consequently, I didn't lose much sleep worrying about whether what I was doing made a difference. The extent to which what one does can be objectively detached from who one is may be debated. But I think that who one is, is where differences really count.

One of the stated measures of merit in the academy is whether one makes a contribution to knowledge; that is, discovers some bit of trivia that hadn't yet been known. I uncovered a bit of minutiae about molecular mechanisms. The ripples on the surface of knowledge are long gone. It was big stuff in those heady days during my tenure among the acclaimed intelligentsia. But I don't think my trivia about molecules will impress anybody reading my obituary, much less the Gate Keeper awaiting my arrival.

I do hope the postscript can honestly say, "He was good to people."

FEBRUARY 27

Life is a Poem

Pat's first teaching position was teaching English at our small-town high school. It was my younger brother Don's senior year and he was enrolled in Pat's course in English literature. For an assignment in a study of poetry the students were to create a short original poem. Don's submission was the following ditty:

Little fly upon the wall,
Him got no Mama, no Mama at all.
Him got no Mama to comb him hair.
Him no care. Him got no hair.

The poem impressed Pat, and Don received her commendation. It fell to me to gently inform Pat that Don's little limerick was not original. I attempted to convince her that it was mine, but she had been alerted to the family's follies. It was part of our family's poetical lore acquired along the way with Jack and Jill and other rhymes.

Unlike Don, I didn't have a pretty, young, English teacher. Consequently, I don't remember much formal exposure to poetry. I do have a sketchy recollection of having to decide what The Sandpiper by Celia Thaxter was all about. My naive assumption that it was about sandpipers didn't impress that teacher. "Unimaginative," she said. What I now know about poetry is largely from brief sporadic excursions into the genre as a no-longer-young adult, motivated mostly as relief from the certainty of scientific punditry. >>>

I have my favorites. I like the rhymes and rhythms of Edgar Allen Poe, and the images of Carl Sandburg. When I read Emily Dickinson's lines, I sense that I have been there too. I have written much about life as a story, sometimes as drama, but never until now did I think of my life as a poem. I wonder how it would read as a poem. Perhaps had I been less indifferent to verse early on I could see the poetry in life.

On the other hand, I can't think of Don's poem being about more than an orphaned fly having a bad hair day.

March

MARCH 1

Old Guy

Yesterday a friend, a bit younger than I, greeted me with "Hello, old guy." As he was stating the obvious, I gave little thought to the nature of his greeting. Thinking about it later, however, I began to wonder about the innuendo of salutations calling attention to age. While to greet an oldster with "Hi, young man" may seem facetious, I am quite sure that "Hey, old guy" or "Hey, old man" have no intrinsic pejorative intent. But I have become curious about the silent, cultural, attitudinal or prejudicial content of statements referring to age. I have noticed that it is much less politically acceptable to say, "Hi, old woman" than it is to say, "Hi, old man." But I digress.

In my ruminations about this, which may reveal some disquiet with attitudes about my demographic cohort, I remembered a brief early morning conversation near my professorial office with a student from Thailand whose father, not coincidentally, had also been a student in my classes. Having momentarily forgotten his name, I greeted him with "Good morning, young man."

"Good morning, old man," he said without hesitation as he walked by. Then with a hint of apology he explained that in his culture "old man" was a title of respect and dignity, but he was uncertain about what it implied in our culture and was fearful that he may have offended me. He had noticed that even though I was approaching the demographic entitlement, only a few disgruntled American students called me "old man."

I am not sure of the point of all this except to say that I much prefer the inference of frivolity in old guy over the cultural innuendos of old man.

MARCH 2

Gramom

These days one hears a lot about parenting skills. It is assumed that there is some objective list of talents that characterize good or better parents and by which a person's relationship with their kids might be measured. One might wonder whether these abilities are innate or learned. I am not aware of any formal educational schemes teaching parenting. The ability is not unlike riding a bicycle. The learning is in the doing, which unfortunately may be too late for some kids. I believe, however, the final analysis of how well one has done in this endeavor ought to be left to the children. Rules or skills notwithstanding, I think parenting is about establishing healthy, enduring relationships.

And then, there is the matter of grandparenting—a phenomenon that provides new avenues of inquiry for the abstracters. My exit lane recollections about my Danish grandfather surface in my mind less frequently now. In most of the ten years that our lives overlapped, he lived in our house—actually his house. I remember being in his presence, but we hardly had a relationship. I can conjure no conversation with him. I'd like to think he liked me. But, in retrospect, I remember a rather indifferent, old-world curmudgeon. My other grandparents, deceased before my time, are largely abstractions. I missed not having had a real, live grandmother. I envy Pat's experiences with her grandmother, which brings me to the point of all this blurbing about grandparents. >>>

It has been my extreme good fortune to watch the unfolding of what must be the quintessence of grandparenting. Pat effortlessly embodies what I am convinced God intended grandmothers to be. Her embrace of our grandkids, both figuratively and literally has been fascinating to observe. Without indulging them she tends to their moods, needs, and wants. She is simply, without condition, there for them. Her counsel is quiet, easy and wise—the epitome of grace, love and understanding. Our down-the-street grandkids come by just to 'hang' with Gramom. You get the picture—the Gramom every kid should have. I marvel at it all and wonder how she came to know that's what grandparenting was meant to be.

Probably learned it from her grandmother.

MARCH 3

Little Thinker

Elsewhere in this muddle of memories about which I have been writing while cruising the exit lane, there is a reference to a boyhood moniker assigned to me by my grandfather. That account hints at some remorse about not knowing why he called me the professor. Probably he noticed a tendency to think abstractly, I reasoned in retrospect.

Being retired with time to ponder matters that probably don't matter much, I have been searching my memory files for some insight about that brief but apparently significant influence in my life. As I recall, it was early in my literary and intellectual development when I would have been exposed to nursery rhymes, probably at age five. Could I have discovered the difference between simply learning nursery rhymes and thinking about them?

Because our house lacked running water we were often sent, like Jack and Jill, to fetch some water. Our well was at the bottom of the hill, however. While I am sure we may have spilled some water, I don't recall any us of falling down or breaking anything. Who falls up anyway? And then there is that business about crowns. There's no hint of Jack's royalty so the fractured crown may just as well have been cranial, not ceremonial at all. My grandfather didn't know—but then, after all, he was Danish.

Humpty Dumpty had a great fall. I still wonder whether the fall was figurative or literal. What caused his descent is unclear, but it is certain that whatever was broken couldn't be fixed, at least not by the resources available. Inasmuch as there were no actual entities matching my images of Humpty Dumpty, I may have assumed the poem was about incompetency in government. Granddad would have liked that. He had been kicked out of Denmark because of his resistance to governmental labor policy.

Why in the world was Jack hurdling fires in the first place? Without electricity in our house we burned a lot of candles, but it never occurred to us to jump over them. Abstaining from such activity and avoiding burns to one's derriére is a good lesson to have learned early. Nobody pointed that out. I learned that all by myself.

Granddad could have noticed.

MARCH 4

Defrocked

There are common stereotypic images that are evoked by the word *professor*. Ordinary folks not acquainted with real live professors tend to think of them pejoratively, as in dull, absent-minded, preoccupied, detached, eccentric and living mostly in the non-real world of abstractions. Professorial types see themselves as bright, erudite, scholarly, meritorious, eminent, etcetera. Most professors I have known, in addition to thinking what they do is necessary, are at one time or another all of the above.

Unlike other professionals, professors when moved to the periphery of productive life are given special emeritus status. (Status is important to professors.) I am unsure about what significance, if any, accrues to one with a title that indicates one is a 'has been,' or what society's expectations are of one no longer licensed to pontificate. I doubt that many professors think of the title emeritus as an "out-of-business" sign reminding themselves and others that what they think probably doesn't matter.

I wonder how many retired professors have forgotten the struggles they encountered when attempting to convince a roomful of colleagues in whose best interests it was to think otherwise. While the defense of intellectual high ground was exciting and challenging, yesterday as I completed the culling of my professional files I found nothing there that would grant me merit in the greater scheme of existence.

There are no professorial ranks in heaven—one of the reasons heaven is heaven.

I won't be buried in my academic regalia. I won't need it there.

MARCH 5

Identity

While searching our bookshelves for a book, another volume of some significance in my personal history caught my attention. Heroes of The 483rd is the title of this outsized tome, a compilation of the activity and personnel of the 483rd Heavy Bombardment Group of the 15th Air Force. The pages display the names and pictures of 2,900 aircrew soldiers who served in air battles over Europe from 1944-1945. I served with that outfit, but my name (no little disappointment) does not appear in that list. Well, it does, but it doesn't. It is misspelled. I don't think I will read the book again.

My father, proud of his Norwegian heritage, took Sti-en as his American name. It was the name of the place in Norway where he was born. He taught me well to be proud of the name and to be suspicious of persons who couldn't learn to spell or pronounce it correctly. My life has been a major crusade against the multitudes, carelessly indifferent to my identity, who say "Stien - Stein - whatever" when I insist that my name is STIEN. It is not that I don't know who I am—it's that I would like for other folks to agree.

I don't think of myself as a hero. My encounters with the enemy were mostly skirmishes. The major battles had occurred before I arrived. However, my only chance to be identified with a bunch of legitimate heroes was botched by an indifferent copy editor who typed Stein into the record and confused my identity as a soldier. >>>

That was then. Now, near the end of the run, my major concern is that whoever calls "The Roll Up Yonder" gets it right!

MARCH 10

Mail Order Dreams

Not unlike most days, our mailbox was crammed with mail order catalogues. I affirm free enterprise and understand that advertising motivates much of consumer spending, but I am annoyed by the invasion of privacy that blatantly attends unsolicited mail. I glance casually at the stuff, peruse very little of it, and find not much I need or want. It has been said this onslaught of junk mail is my own fault. I am told that if I had never sent an order I would have been spared the barrage. But paper addressed to Resident still accumulates and I fume at the imposed obligation to carry it off to the recycling center.

During our depression-stricken and drought-riddled existence in the dirty thirties, I spent hours buried in the pages of the Sears-Roebuck catalogue wishing for things I thought I needed. Now, by contrast, there is little that interests me in these catalogues. Then the disposal of an outdated catalogue was simple. Its pragmatic fate was preordained before it ever arrived in our rural mailbox.

There is one omission in the current catalogue caper that annoys me a bit, however. There are no fashions designed to enhance the countenance of near elderly fellows modeled by handsome, well-preserved, white-haired guys like me. I can guess at the rationale for that. Either there aren't enough of us to bother about or it's a shrinking market with little chance of repeating sales, inasmuch as the clothes we now wear will probably outlast us. >>>

But what can be wrong with a little fuel for the fantasies of those of us whose early sartorial aspirations were nurtured by an out-back perusal of a Sears-Roebuck catalogue?

MARCH 12

Poking Along

When we were kids, in the first quarter of the last century, we listened to our Dad's collection of Victrolla records on his hand-cranked Edison phonograph. Among them was a recording called "The Sunday Drivers." The song was about the carefree days in the twenties when the emergence of the automobile had progressed so recreational driving became an option. "Got no lights; got no brakes— we're the Sunday drivers" was the refrain. I can still whistle the melody, if anyone is interested.

Today was Sunday, another day of rest in this cycle of days, and Pat and I went out for a bit of recreational driving. Not to any place in particular nor to some place else, just a bit of Sunday driving. Recreational driving isn't like it once was. Most driving today is about where one is going and not much about the journey. Driving for the fun of it is mostly off the road in off-the-road, heavy duty, all-wheel-drive vehicles or wide-tired motorbikes. I got my off-the-road thrills operating tractors or combines on the steep slopes of the Palouse wheat fields.

Actually, leisurely Sunday driving in the family sedan is riskier than the off-the-road stuff. People in a hurry to someplace else have little patience with unhurried folks enjoying the scenery. We are urged along with honking horns, tail-gating, dangerous maneuvers, or some single phalangeal gestures. Sure, poking along hesitantly is an annoyance, but it's usually the intolerance of others that makes it dangerous.

When quizzed about what adjustments are required of oldsters making their way in retirement, I have been heard to answer, "Staying out of the way." But I wasn't speaking about Sunday driving. There ought to be some room for folks who have earned the right to poke along and enjoy the rest of the journey.

After all, was it not our generation that built the roads?

MARCH 15
I Didn't Do It

Occasionally I meander onto the campus of my professorial alma mater to see what's changed. What hasn't changed, I discovered today, is the predilection of professors to categorize people, usually in hierarchies of three and not unusually with a touch of satire or judgment. For example, those who make things happen - those who watch things happen - those who say, "what happened?"

That categorization, originally meant to satirize a hierarchy of merit, virtue, or worth in some enterprise, now seems to me could be made to represent not only professors but also folks in general. Whenever I read or hear one of these attempts to classify folks, I confess wondering to which class I belong.

When professionally active I, like most professors, instinctively put myself in the first of the above categories. I assumed I made things happen, but never made lists of what I thought I caused to happen.

Now that I have retired and have time to think more clearly about this nonsense, whatever list I might have made would have been quite short and not particularly impressive. I am convinced now that I, like all my professorial cohorts, actually functioned more often in the group that was trying to figure out what was happening.

The notion that professors by definition are the prestigious group assigned to make things happen still surfaces in my musing. It is being subdued, however, by the growing suspicion that I may have stayed too long in the profession with all of its airs, when there were these more exciting things to do— like being retired and watching things happen.

And being glad none of it is my fault.

MARCH 16

Birthday Thoughts

I've been trying to sort out the paradox of life seeming to be both cyclic and linear. Maybe life is just one big or small (but big sounds better) wheel and it only goes around so many times and then stops right where it started. You know, sort of like dust to dust—and we use birthdays as a way of reminding ourselves that we have a long way yet to go or that we are almost there. Then different birthdays have different functions as we go merrily rolling along. Who was it that said, "What goes around comes around?" It was either Adam or Aristotle. Probably it was Aristotle. The only recorded words of Adam were his conversations with God, and in those he was making excuses. (This is getting interesting.)

Or maybe life is a road and birthdays are resting places along the way where one is invited to stop and wonder about (among other things) whether life is cyclic or linear. The Bible tells about a lot of roads—to Jericho, to Emmaus, to Jerusalem—and it tells about some that are narrow and some that are broad. Now it occurs to me that the Bible has more to say about roads than it does about wheels. So maybe that's the answer—life is linear! And birthdays are, indeed, wayside stops where we are invited to pause and wonder in awe about the miracle of life and marvel at the grace of God and give thanks for it all.

Do you suppose God in His wisdom knew that we would likely get so busy living that we would not take time to marvel at the wonder of life and He invented birthdays as a kind of special invitation to pause and rest and celebrate his goodness? After all, it was the birthday of His Son about which the Bible says the most. And that, indeed, was a celebration.

So I pause at this, your birthday, to gives thanks to God for you, especially for your cheerful, hopeful, and healthy perspective on life and to celebrate with you one more turn of the wheel along the road of life.

By the way, HAPPY BIRTHDAY!

MARCH 17

A Birthday

Hey Beth, ever wonder why we make so much of one's birthday? After all it's just one of the 365 days one lives each year. And it doesn't come around any more frequently than any of the others. It is true for each of us that particular day is the very first day of our very first year. So in that sense I suppose it indicates some kind of starting place and, having done that, it becomes a point of reference for all the rest of our days each year. And do you wonder why, except for a bit more attention, we should expect the day to be happier than the other 364 days of our year? I wouldn't want for anyone to have an unhappy birthday, but perhaps one might consider trading a not-so-happy birthday for a few more happy days in between.

I remember some of my childhood birthdays, being confused about how I was to respond to expressions of love and wishes for good fortune when I seldom experienced that kind of stuff during the other days of my year. It may be that our human tendency to ritualize our expressions of love, gratitude and appreciation causes us to depend on ceremony to accomplish what should be a way of living each day. We attempt to cram a whole year's worth of love and affection into one day and then be casual or negligent the rest of the year, like going to church and praising God on Sunday and being insensitive or indifferent to his presence on the other days of the week. >>>

That's not how it is with your birthday. Your birthday is a reminder that on one special day of 1959 God gave to us the other special child we wanted. And on each birthday of yours since then, I remember not only that day but all the days in-between those birthdays. The gift goes on. Each birthday we participate in the ritual, not only because that's the way we do things in this society but because each of your days, since we began counting, is a part of an immeasurable gift that makes us glad.

Your birthday reminds us of that.

MARCH 18

Passed By

I am among a shrinking remnant born at the edge of a horse-powered, pre-electricity society, which gave way to automobiles, tractors, diesel-electric locomotives, radios, airplanes, telephones, and rural electrification. Electrical power was still competing with steam when coal-burning, steam locomotives powered many of the troop trains I traveled on during World War II. Our farmhouse had neither electric lights nor indoor plumbing. When I mention the era to my grandchildren, they say from the driver's seat of their Civics with a cell phone in one ear and an iPod in the other "We know— you walked to and from school in the dark, against the wind, uphill both ways, knee-deep in snow." And we did homework by kerosene lamps, I remind them. "Oh, we thought it was candlelight," they tease.

Now I watch with wonder the digital, wireless, virtual, other world in which they live. With cell phones, e-mail, X-boxes, IM, iPods, Googling, blogging, twittering, YouTube, and FaceBook, they don't ever have to enter the real world. I am falling behind both the language and the barrage of gadgets of their culture. All they need yet is a Star Trek type food-replicator and a de-replicator to deal with real waste.

It is disconcertingly easy for us oldsters to feel being passed by. I don't begrudge them their gadgets; I both admire and envy their technological savvy. But I wonder about their self-imposed isolation from the world of real things like the fragrance of flowers, the warmth of personal contact, gentle breezes, non-digital real nature, the affectionate touch of a loving hand, the view out of the window, or a walk on the beach with the sound of real waves unadulterated by iPod noise.

Who is being passed by, I wonder.

MARCH 19

Spring Has Sprung

Seasons of weather are often used analogously in comments about one's trek through life. Spring, a period of awakening and growth. Summer, a time for adventure and excitement. Fall, time to button up or dig in. And Winter, to settle in and wait it out. The analogy between the gray skies of winter and the gravitas of the winter of life becomes strained with the realization that one of those scenarios is cyclic and the other is not. But this bit of recall is not about winter, neither literal nor figurative. It's about spring.

Memories conjured by my trek along the exit lane have become peculiarly seasonal. Risking innuendos of senility, I am not at all apologetic about my penchant for reminiscing. I have concluded that memories that linger are the good stuff of life worth reliving.

It's been said that in springtime a young man's fancy turns to thoughts of love. I don't know of any comparable phrase about what happens to an old man's springtime thoughts. Mine seem to have turned to Burma Shave slogans.

Springtime conjures delightful memories about boyhood school days. We, my siblings and I, walked two miles home from school when weather permitted. After the snow melted and mild temperatures arrived we shed our long underwear, our four-buckle overshoes, and heavy woolen coats. So lightened we sauntered along two miles of country road enjoying warm breezes, spring flowers and green grass. As we neared our farmstead, we would walk by a series of five signs attached to our pig-pasture fence posts displaying safety slogans and, not coincidentally, advertising Burma Shave shaving cream. The signs were changed periodically. The following are some that appeared on the fence posts of our pasture and linger in the recesses of my mind:

Drove too long - driver snoozing - what happened next - was not amusing.   BURMA SHAVE

Speed was high - weather was hot - tires were thin - X marks the spot.   BURMA SHAVE

The midnight ride - of Paul for beer - led to a warmer hemisphere.   BURMA SHAVE

At intersections - look each way - a harp sounds nice - but it's hard to play.   BURMA SHAVE

Spring has sprung - the grass has rizz - where last year's - careless driver is!   BURMA SHAVE

It was the latter that surfaced in my mind and turned my thoughts to Burma Shave (and spring) when Grandson Jesse said this morning, "Looks like spring is here, Granddad."

Nothing wrong with my mind.

MARCH 20

Default Setting

It has been said that an intellectual is one who doesn't think about sex all of the time. I am not aware of definitions of *intellectual* to which everyone agrees. Certainly the above statement is not one of them, but it does raise questions about how one manages one's thoughts; that is, what determines the content of a person's mental activity apart from that which is essential to the ongoing functioning of one's body. A toe jammed against furniture tends to focus one's thoughts sharply away from appetites or abstractions. Once the agony subsides the brain will pick up whatever it was doing before the crisis.

When the physical apparatus is running smoothly and the brain relieved from tending to the business of making a living, the excess expendable neural capacity turns to thinking; that is, the default setting seems to be thinking with possibly a link to thinking about thinking. That is what has happened to me at this moment and I am wondering how it happened.

Apparently the brain can't idle. It just cannot do nothing. There was a brief time after I retired when I immodestly proclaimed that I had mastered doing nothing. But I have come to realize that, short of outright dying, one cannot *not* be doing something. Perhaps one might sit or lie perfectly still with a blank, unblinking stare, all of which actually requires some focused brain activity. The only way to nothingness is to have someone pull the plug. > > >

I have become increasingly curious about what goes on in the minds of idle, quiescent, old folks. They have to be thinking about something even if it is only thinking about getting older. When that stops, getting older is over.

Now that I think about it, even thinking about nothing is doing something. All this nattering about the impossibility of doing nothing makes me wonder if it is possible to write something about nothing.

I think I may have done just that. It shouldn't take long to read this.

MARCH 22

Old Tapes

The 22nd of March stands out in my index of days as one for which the memories are more indelibly etched than almost any other in what has become a rather lengthy list. The particular March 22nd of which I write came early in my accrual of days. It was March 22, 1945, the day of my initiation into the realities of war. The tradition that real heroes do not talk much about their heroics probably constrains most veterans from exposing their memories in any detail, if at all. It may follow then that guys who do are not true heroes. That debate is for another time.

This is not just about memories, but also my curiosity about the stability of memory. Too much chatter about memories risks the indictment of living in the past, but paradoxically one cannot leave one's past behind. Some memories of extreme experiences seem to move nearer the surface as time passes. It is not uncommon for younger generations to hear repeated renditions of intense memories by their oldsters, which often appear more vivid than last week's birthday party. My mother in her 85th year would remember when as a teenager she discovered the body of a murdered neighbor more clearly than my most recent visit.

This brings me again to March 22, 1945, the day of my very first bomber mission over Germany. I was 18 years old, curious, scared, and alone at the tail end of the plane, fascinated with the expanding puffs of smoke from exploding anti-aircraft shells. The bomber 100 feet to our right, still loaded with bombs, was obliterated by a direct hit. Terrified, I watched as the aircraft along with the nine crewmen, engulfed in enormous black and orange flames, disintegrated. I could only watch and ponder the meaning of it all. I remember thinking there has to be a better way.

It doesn't require much scrutiny of the memory banks to conjure the vivid images of those flames, but I don't often think, much less talk, about that day in March. But then I don't talk much about what transpired on the 22nd of last month.

That I don't remember.

MARCH 25
Sundays

A life span of eighty years includes 4,171 Sundays. Obviously there is also the same number of Saturdays, as well as all the other days of the week. Without a detailed 80-year diary one can't recall with any certainty one's activity on each of the 4,171 reoccurrences of any one of the weekly cycling days. If I were asked what I did on the 139th Saturday of my earthly sojourn, my answer would be, "I have no idea." However, if I were asked the same question about my 139th Sunday, I could say with some assurance that I had gone to church or was taken there by my parents. The first officially recorded appearance of my presence in church was one of the Sundays of April in 1926. I was baptized along with my twin brother that April Sunday in the oldest Lutheran church in rural western Minnesota.

Of course, I don't remember it, but I do have a document that testifies to the event. My parents introduced me (and my siblings) to church and its doctrines early. While a youth I was instructed in the belief systems of the Lutheran church and given answers to questions I had not yet asked. Because I correctly answered the questions at confirmation on one of the Sundays of April in 1938, completely marinated in Lutheran-ism, I was awarded full membership in the Lutheran Church. There is more to the story but I am still reviewing that.

Why this reminiscence about my church history? As I sat in church today listening to the preacher, it occurred to me to wonder how many sermons I had survived since that momentous April day, now 80 years ago. Whether anyone has been keeping score or whether merits accrue to one listening to sermons does not concern me much. Hearing them is another issue. One can hear a lot just by listening, my grandfather would say.

But I can say with confidence where I was on the majority of the 4,171 Sundays in my fourscore-year allotment.

MARCH 28

Dear Mom

Several months ago my daughter gave me a book entitled WAR LETTERS. The book is a compilation of letters written by World War II soldiers to family members back home. About that same time my sister sent me a packet of letters that I had written to my mother (a few to my father) during my tenure as a soldier in the States and in Italy during the final months of the war. Yesterday while culling files I came upon letters (e-mails actually) I have received from grandson Jordan in the sandbox, his designation of his whereabouts in his war. Rereading Jordan's notes motivated me to revisit my letters to my mother.

I was eighteen years old when most of the letters were penned. They had been secured in my mother's trove for nearly sixty years before they fell again into my hands. In contrast to the letters in WAR LETTERS— revealing the intensity of fear and loneliness, the devastation of life, body and spirit, the physical pain of wounds, emotional hurt of infidelity and the bewildering uncertainty of it all— my letters are quite bland. They would never be included in a collection intended to expose the dark realities war. When I came to the arena the major battles were done. Except for a couple of fierce battles in which I witnessed danger, death, and destruction, my sorties (while involving scores of bombers) were minor skirmishes. Strangely there is no mention of any of that or my response to it in any of my letters. I had no heroics about which to write. >>>

My letters leave the impression that I wrote and received a lot of letters. One note tells of a day I received twenty-five letters. But reading mine tells little about what was going on in my head. In retrospect, that's surprising given my proclivity to introspection. There are many references to letters I had received but little about what they said. Some were from people I have no recollection of writing to or receiving letters from.

I had never read through those letters to Mom before. I suppose I did before I mailed them, but not since. I recall setting them aside after I had read a few because I was dismayed at the incorrect grammar, casual spelling, and general immaturity of thought. I remember being more sophisticated.

I have to believe Mom cherished the letters. She kept them the rest of her life.

MARCH 29

What's New?

After the customary exchange of greetings, an acquaintance of mine whom I hadn't seen recently seemed eager to extend the conversation. He asked, "What's new in your life?" giving me permission to talk about myself. That is not something that I, a reticent Norwegian, am naturally inclined to do. I really don't know which is preferable, to talk at length about me or listen to others talk at length about themselves. I always struggle with what I might say about myself that would be of interest to anyone. If he had said, " How are you?" I most likely would have assumed he was anxious about my health or perhaps even my moral well-being. Fortunately, he didn't ask that. I quite likely would have replied without any embellishment that I was well and put the ball back in play on his side of the net.

But he had asked, "What's new?" My first thought was that's not a fair question to ask an old guy. We are all much better prepared to talk about what's old. There is so much more old in our lives than there is new, or perhaps the wheel has gone around so many times that every new thing seems deja vu. The Bible seems to agree. The wise man of Ecclesiastes writes: Is *there anything of which one can say, look this is something new? What has been will be again; what has been done will be done again; there is nothing new under the sun.*

While it is true that our world has a way of making new things old, I am quite sure my friend wasn't expecting a lecture on Old Testament wisdom when he asked, "What's new?" I think he wanted to carry on a bit of conversation with someone he had not seen for awhile, most likely so that when he told his wife he had spoken with me he would have something to say when she asked, "So, what's new with him?"

That's what Pat asked me when I told her that I saw Joe this morning.

April Again

APRIL 1
Mother Goose's Gander

In these days of repose to keep my mind occupied and to stay out of the way, I spend considerable time at the keyboard of my iMac. By nature a highly introspective person, my mind is always busy but much of the busyness is idle rumination, the content of which is usually interesting, sometimes amusing and worth recording. I indulge myself with the fantasy that if I do this often enough I could become a writer. That fancy usually fades when I ask what's so great about being a writer, but I am still convinced that writing is as good for one's mind as it is for one's soul. So I persist. Sustaining a healthy mind and a healthy soul may be, after all, what the Psalmist meant by numbering one's days.

I am constantly surprised by how little of the accumulated stuff once preeminent in my mind about biological paradigms surfaces in my daily musing about life in the exit lane. I am more apt to find myself curious about why Mother Goose rhymes persist. I do worry that musing about the words of childhood poetry might indicate the ominous onset of senile dementia.

Nevertheless, there is wisdom in that genre that strangely becomes too easily mixed with imagery of other stuff sequestered in my mental store. For example, I was tracing sequences of thought drifting through my head when I came onto the lines, *Mother Goose flies through the air on the wings of a very fine gander*. What I hadn't learned when a child was that Mother Goose wasn't a goose at all but a witch, but I do remember wondering how a goose could write all those rhymes. That she had a gander didn't surprise me because I learned in biology class that in real life, every goose does indeed have a gander. Wild geese, like many avian species, mate for life and in many cases the female is the dominant mate. She calls the shots, which may or may not have any relevance to current sociological notions about gender roles. One could say that this goose and gander thing started with Adam and Eve, but that might be making metaphors without merit—a mix of biology, Bible, and nursery rhymes.

Some senescence here?

APRIL 3

Approved

Early in my tenure as a classroom teacher I learned the reasons that motivate students to enroll in college courses are as numerous and as varied as the students registered. Some courses are required by an academic program. "My major mandates it" or "It is a general college requirement," students would say. Or "I want to get it out of the way so I can get on with the interesting stuff." Not the most expedient thing to say to one's biology professor,

Students are too easily influenced by counseling from their peers. They rate courses as hard or easy, or more often tag professors as hard or easy. It's acceptable to avoid a course because the prof is hard, but less so to admit enrolling in a course because it is easy. The latter is tantamount to confessing questionable academic adequacy.

It was my practice at the beginning of a course to encourage students to talk about why they appeared in my classroom. Because it was required was the reason most frequently stated, followed next by having been encouraged to do so by their advisor, another professor, a parent, a roommate, a boy or girl friend.

My intent in these brief deliberations was to convince them to consider my preferred reason, which was to learn biology. Scores of students will remember my insistence that no worldview is complete without some understanding of biology, and I hoped that would be their primary motivation for coming to class.

What this is really all about is one student's unforgettable response to the question about why he had enrolled in my legendary Bioscience course.

Following one of these discussions he privately announced (not at all facetiously) that Jesus had told him to register for my course. I asked him if he had any idea of the pressure that put on both him and me. Six weeks later he dropped the course, which required his advisor's signature. I reluctantly signed the drop-slip.

He hadn't secured his advisor's approval.

APRIL 5

A Sad Day

While I can't recall a specific occasion, I am sure I have wept at times during recent months. But today I, not given to excessive sentiment, sobbed without inhibition or embarrassment. Today was a sad day. Knickers, our resident West Highland terrier who had been happily cruising the exit lane with us, came to the red light at the end of the off-ramp. His demise, though not unexpected, came abruptly. It was a cheerless day for which I was unprepared—and I wept.

I don't know whether my tears were for Knick or for me, but the sadness was mine. He came to stay with us when his family no longer had space worthy of his quiet, but lively dignified presence. For three hundred days he charmed our household and visitors to the round house. Those were, indeed, days that counted. I had become glad for his undemanding, carefree, delightful company. We, he and I, walked the streets in the neighborhood and hiked the trails in the wooded hills beyond, where I savored the scenery of the country side and he relished the sniffery of the pathways.

Knickers (in doggy days) was an octogenarian like me. But I knew him when he was a young dog in Minnesota. When we visited his family there, he invited me on lengthy treks around Lake Como. He was pleasant and patient with strollers in the park but mildly indifferent to canine cohorts. Although I envied the attention he received, I felt a bit regal when I accompanied him about the metropolis, even though folks seldom noticed the other end of his leash. >>>

In recent weeks his innards failed to sustain him and he wasted in size and vitality, but not in spirit. Our walks become shorter and slower. His interest in people diminished and his indifference to dogs intensified, but he insisted on lingering at spots of deep olfactory interest. His favorite places of repose are empty now. He was an uncannily quiet fellow. He barked only when a raccoon or coyote passed the premises. Still the place seems strangely silent now.

We will miss him dreadfully.

APRIL 9

The Long Wait

When asked what I have been writing these days I usually simply say, "Blurbs." The word blurb is not common in the speaking vocabulary of many folks. Most assume that I am referring to blogging, currently a fashionable Internet activity. I have acquired a fondness for the word *blurb* as well as the writing of blurbs, which I call *blurbing*—not to be confused with blurting or blabbing, a.k.a. blogging.

I had been ambivalent about how to refer to my daily jotting about life in extra innings until I chanced upon *blurb*. While not commonly used and generally considered to be slang, the word carries the distinct connotation of commendation or praise. After reflecting on these bits of reflection I think *blurb* is the right choice, inasmuch as the days counted or recounted in this endeavor have been good days.

A lingering uncertainty about this writing caper, which began as a daily exercise to keep my fourth-quarter mind alert, is how much closer, if any, the routine has moved me towards the Gates of Wisdom about which the Psalmist wrote.

Teach us to number our days that we may enter the gate of wisdom is how one modern translation states the promise. I find nothing in the account about how soon into the practice one should begin to sense signs of wisdom. It hasn't happened yet. I am suspicious that The Gates of Wisdom may just be another name for The Pearly Gates.

If so, I may just have to wait.

APRIL 10

Postlogue - The Last Word

My colleague, Dave, was a man ahead of the times. Trained in the science of ecology he was our college's environmental conscience, calling attention to our use and abuse of the natural physical context in which we humans exist long before it became fashionable or imperative to do so. "If we are in a contest with Nature we are destined to lose," he would say, "because Nature wrote the rules and gets to bat last—or have the last word."

In this day-counting endeavor I have only hinted at what lies beyond the red light at the end of the off ramp. That is an arena about which we believe more than we know. And those images are badly blurred. Exit lane. Extra innings. Overtime. Fourth Quarter. All analogous inferences to nearing the end of the journey do not address the question about what comes after the counting is over.

If the scoffers who argue that that there is no God and life is an unfortunate joke perpetrated by an uncaring universe are right, they may have the last word—but I wonder to whom they will speak it. If the believers who insist that life (in this time and space and existence beyond here and now) is one continuous saga are right, they may have the last word. But I expect them to have bowed heads, standing in the awesome presence of God in reverent silence.

I have placed my bet with the believers. The pages that inspire my hope speak of a reality, albeit cloaked in mystery, where God will meet both those who journeyed in expectation and those who traveled in indifference. Given the awesome majesty of God, I don't expect a lot of chatter. If I do, indeed, stand with the awestruck multitude, it will not be because of anything I have done.

It will be because of what He has done. The last word is His.

Index

DESTINY

Having Fun Yet? . . . . Jan 4
Reciprocity . . . . Jan 23
The Off Ramp . . . . Feb 25
Statistical Disquiet . . . . . May 11
My Donkey . . . . May 16
Remembering Me . . . . . . July 25
Symptoms . . . . Aug 28
Two Roads . . . . Sept 4
A Reminder . . . . Nov 1
The Record . . . . Dec 7
Expectations. . . . . Dec 22

GENERATIONS

Hats Off. . . . . Jan 12
Different . . . . Jan 24
Genes & Generations. . . . . Jan 27
A Premonition. . . . . Feb 2
The Other End. . . . . Feb 3
Gramom. . . . . March 2
Little Thinker. . . . . March 3
A Birthday. . . . . March 17
Dear Mom . . . . March 28
Stumped. . . . . April 16
A Gene from Mom. . . . . April 26
Files. . . . . May 5
Brothers Five. . . . . May 9

The Willow Switch. . . . . May 17
For Beth . . . . May 31
Abbie . . . . June 17
Father's Day. . . . . June 18
As the Wheel Turns. . . . June 28
The Box . . . . July 4
Ramshackle Dreams . . . . . July 19
Flies . . . . Aug 1
Red Wagon. . . . . Aug 12
Genealogy . . . . Aug 14
Gran'dogs . . . . Aug 27
Shadows. . . . . Sept 8
Ancestors. . . . . Sept 14
Untold Story. . . . . Nov 3
Goodbye, Good Brother. . . Dec 29

IDENTITY

Reflections . . . . Jan 14
Who? . . . . Feb 4
Little Old Man . . . . Feb 11
My Numbers . . . . Feb 15
My Mirror & Me . . . . Feb 20
Identity . . . . March 3
Old Tapes . . . . March 22
What's New? . . . . March 29
In the Beginning. . . . . April 11
Dismissed . . . . April 21
By Any Other Name . . . April 30
A Perfect Day . . . . June 2

445

Gross Anatomy . . . . June 24
Rigs & Rigness . . . . July 8
I Gotta Be Me . . . . July 27
Lost in Thought . . . . Sept 1
What If? . . . . Sept 3
Unforgettable . . . . Sept 10
The Real Story . . . . Sept 21
No Kings Named . . . . Sept 23
Some New Thing. . . . . . . Sept 25
Postscripts . . . . Sept 27
Ain't Gonna Study. . . . . . Nov 11
Seesaw Memories. . . . . . . .Nov 13
Signs. . . . . .Nov 26
Obitus. . . . . .Dec 5
Public Education . . . . Dec 21

OBSERVATIONS

Ogling. . . . . Feb 8
Dream Come True. . . . . . . Feb 12
Looking Good. . . . . .Feb 13
It Was Different Then. . . .Feb 23
Life is a Poem. . . . . Feb 27
Poking Along. . . . . March 12
I Didn't Do It. . . . . March 15
Birthday Thoughts. . . . March 16
Default Setting. . . . . . . March 20
Free Stuff. . . . . .April 27
Symphonic Subtlety . . . . May 13
Remembering. . . . . .May 28

Throwaway Days. . . . . June 1
The Day After . . . . July 5
Trucks. . . . . August 8
Nobody. . . . . Sept 7
Making Lists. . . . . Sept 28
Rainy Day. . . . . Sept 29
Soot is OK. . . . . Oct 3
Intellectual Grazing. . . . . . .Oct 7
Ethnic Eccentricity. . . . . . Oct 30
Impatient Patients . . . . . . Nov 30

OLDER NOW

Do Not Bend . . . . Jan 9
It's Not Funny . . . . Jan 26
After Work . . . . .Jan 28
Get Over It . . . . Jan 31
Keeping Busy . . . . Feb 18
Old Guy . . . . March 1
Mail Order Dreams . . . March 10
Passed By. . . . . March 18
Mother Goose's. . . . April Again 1
A Sad Day . . . . April Again 5
Actuarial Reality . . . . . . .April 14
Senectitude . . . . .April 28
Downsizing Dogma . . . . . .July 6
Geezers, etcetera . . . . July 23
Extra Innings . . . . Aug 15
Paradox of Progress . . . . . Aug 20
Thanks for. . . . . Sept 15

446

Still Driving . . . . Sept 16
Nothing to Say . . . . Oct 1
Final Steps . . . . Oct 5
No Song To Sing . . . . Oct 11
Old or Older . . . . Oct 27
Hanging . . . . Oct 29
Life is So Retro . . . . Nov 16
To Do or Not To Do . . . . . Dec 6

PEOPLE & PLACES

Insignificance . . . . Jan 11
Affirmation . . . . Jan 17
Untied . . . . Feb 9
An Unfaithful Friend . . . . . Feb 22
Spring has Sprung . . . . . . March 19
Hey, Smokey . . . . April 13
Eating Crow . . . . June 15
Merlot, Mozart . . . . June 22
Pen Pal . . . . June 26
First Wine . . . . Aug 10
Ancient Ways . . . . Aug 13
Sandbox . . . . Sept 11
Reunions . . . . Sept 12
Hobby Horses . . . . Sept 17
Rellies in the Park . . . . Oct 16
Helga Died Today . . . . Nov 7
Found Out . . . . Nov 15
A Moose or Two . . . . Dec 12
Presumption . . . . Dec 26

PROFESSORIALISMS

Triumph of Triviality . . . . Jan 10
Recovering . . . . Jan 16
What Matters . . . . Feb 26
Defrocked . . . . March 4
Approved . . . . April Again 3
Meritocracy . . . . April 23
Program Notes . . . . May 12
Peripheral Perceptions . . . June 4
Hidden Talent . . . . June 22
Thoughts About . . . . July 16
Duh . . . . Aug 3
Grandfather by Proxy . . . . Dec 1

RELIGION

A Song . . . . Jan 22
Baptism . . . . Feb 19
Sundays . . . . March 25
The Long Wait . . . April Again 9
Postlogue . . . . April Again 10
Paralogue . . . . April 18
Easter . . . . April 20
Divine Diversion . . . . May 14
You Don't Say! . . . . May 29
Solemnity . . . . June 5
Like Him . . . . July 15
A Holy Hello . . . . July 29
Imperfection . . . . Aug 19
The Book . . . . Sept 30

Moving On............... Oct 18
Delinquent............... Oct 19
Soulful Reserves......... Oct 23
On Being Tall .... Nov 4
Sermon on the Road..... Nov 10
Who's Counting........ Nov 19
Giving Thanks.......... Nov 24
Desparate Disparity...... Nov 25
Light................... Nov 28
Praise or Worship........ Dec 8
A Christmas Pageant..... Dec 11
Christmas Letters........ Dec 16
Speechless in Seattle..... Dec 19
Thoughts on Christmas.. Dec 25

TOGETHER

Living in the Round .... Jan 5
Culinary Harmony .... Feb 6
Excuses .... Feb 14
Good Guys.............. Feb 17
Pinch Day Poets .... April 12
Near Elderly .... April 15
Musical Potpourri ...... April 19
Out of Nowhere .... May 6
A Birthday .... May 7
Birthday Thoughts ...... May 7
Decades .... May 20
Moved by Time .... May 25

Old Promises .... June 19
Days That Count ..... June 20
Still Counting .... June 21
Broken Circle .... Aug 25

WORDS

Obviosities............. April 17
Too Few Words .... Feb 5
Off the Hook .... May 8
Empty Words .... May 10
Sarpy Creek .... July 20
Nostolgy .... July 24
Neologisms .... July 26
My Words .... Aug 6
Stages of Life .... Sept 24
Unlikely Spots .... Oct 10
Ticks .... Oct 12
It's in the Telling........ Oct 13
Now You Know .... Oct 15
Outings .... Oct 21
A New Word .... Nov 5
Going Home .... Nov 27
Entropy .... Dec 13
Missing Words .... Dec 27

Biography

HOWARD STIEN was born to immigrant Scandinavian parents last century at the twilight of the horse and buggy era. He lived with them on their Minnesota farm until high school graduation, after which he served with the US Army Air Corps in Italy as a tail gunner on a B-17 bomber.

After the war Stien and his wife, Pat, raised wheat and cattle on a marginal North Dakota farm for several years. During winter months there, he taught elementary children in the neighborhood one-room schoolhouse. At age 27 he left the farm for college, intending to become a preacher but on the way became a professor. He held faculty positions as Professor of Biology at several colleges and universities.

To keep perspective on the real world, Stien has engaged in diversional activities over the years, among them ranch work, lay preaching, designing and building houses. Both he and Pat (Professor of Theatre Arts) retired after teaching thirty years at Whitworth College in Spokane where they lived in a round house he built one summer to clear his mind.

In retirement Stien has been writing children's stories and some lampoonery about his life as a professor. This is his third book.